Evergreen

Evergreen

*Cultivate the Enduring Customer Loyalty
That Keeps Your Business Thriving*

NOAH FLEMING

⧸AMACOM

AMERICAN MANAGEMENT ASSOCIATION

New York • Atlanta • Brussels • Chicago • Mexico City • San Francisco
Shanghai • Tokyo • Toronto • Washington, D.C.

Bulk discounts available. For details visit:
www.amacombooks.org/go/specialsales
Or contact special sales:
Phone: 800-250-5308
E-mail: specialsls@amanet.org
View all the AMACOM titles at: www.amacombooks.org
American Management Association: www.amanet.org

This publication is designed to provide accurate and authoritative information in regard to the subject matter covered. It is sold with the understanding that the publisher is not engaged in rendering legal, accounting, or other professional service. If legal advice or other expert assistance is required, the services of a competent professional person should be sought.

Library of Congress Cataloging-in-Publication Data
Fleming, Noah.
    Evergreen : cultivate the enduring customler loyalty that keeps your business thriving / Noah Fleming.
        pages cm
    Includes index.
    ISBN-13: 978-0-8144-3443-7
    ISBN-10: 0-8144-3443-6
1. Customer relations.   2. Customer loyalty. I. Title.
    HF5415.5.F584 2015
    658.8'12—dc23   2014016981

About AMA
American Management Association (www.amanet.org) is a world leader in talent development, advancing the skills of individuals to drive business success. Our mission is to support the goals of individuals and organizations through a complete range of products and services, including classroom and virtual seminars, webcasts, webinars, podcasts, conferences, corporate and government solutions, business books, and research. AMA's approach to improving performance combines experiential learning—learning through doing—with opportunities for ongoing professional growth at every step of one's career journey.

Printing number
10 9 8 7 6 5 4 3 2 1

This book is dedicated to my wife,
Heather, and our two sweet girls, **Avalon** and **Ella**.

Heather, you were really the main inspiration for this book.
When you agreed to go out with me, I knew I had to learn very quickly
how to nurture and cultivate an Evergreen relationship,
and the real benefits you could gain from retaining your best customer.

Avalon and Ella, you are, quite simply,
the two most beautiful seedlings I've ever known!

CONTENTS

         Back to Life*   203

                Identifying When the Customer Relationship Is Over   205

                Figuring Out Why Customers Leave in the First Place   208

                Solving Your Customer Attrition Problems   212

                Establishing Constant Contact   215

                Building Effective Attrition Alarm Systems   217

                Implementing Your Reactivation System   220

                Managing Your Expectations About Reactivation   225

   11   Bringing In New Customers: *Creating Optimal Growing
         Conditions*   227

                Managing the Expectations Gap   229

                Creating Customer Loyalty with the First Transaction   231

                Onboarding New Customers   234

                Communicating with the Customer After the Honeymoon
                     Is Over   238

                Preparing for a (Hopefully Insanely) Successful Promotion   243

                Afterword: The End Is the Beginning   249

                             Notes   255

                             Index   261

                       About the Author   271

FOREWORD

Los Angeles is a warm-weather creation, at a similar latitude as much of North Africa and Southeast Asia. But whenever I've flown in I've had the feeling it's not as lush as my native northeastern United States. Yet, back home, we routinely endure winters with feet of snow and temperatures below zero. How can that disparity exist?

It exists because L.A. is not verdant. New England is, to a large extent, evergreen. The approaches to L.A. look brown and the approaches to Boston look green—even in winter.

And green is the stuff of life, of photosynthesis, of new growth, of regeneration.

In this remarkable book, Noah Fleming (himself of cold climes warmed by evergreens in our neighbor to the north) explains how your customers and business can eternally provide life, growth, and regeneration. Deciduous trees can be quite attractive, so long as we arrange for those trillions of leaves to be carted away come fall. They add a nice touch, as do transient customers in any business.

But transient customers also must be "cleaned up." They often require more investment than their revenue justifies, and they can disturb the landscape where the evergreens should bloom. The evergreen customer is a constant resource—of business, referrals, goodwill, good ideas, and market power.

Noah explains how customers have to be attracted, nurtured, and retained to create your own verdant, fertile, business landscape. Some require careful tending; others thrive with minimal intervention. Some respond best to light, others to warmth. Not everything grows and prospers in common conditions. It's important to recognize the optimal growth circumstances for your particular environment and customers.

The best firms and influencers I've ever seen know their ideal customers perfectly. They can appeal to them instantly, with total focus and relevance. As a global consultant for more than twenty-five years, I've seen too many great ideas wasted on the wrong people and a great many average ideas succeed brilliantly because they were directed at exactly the right people.

Imagine your products and services directed at the right targets with optimal power? This book shows you how.

I often fly into Boston in the middle of harsh winters, only to see that the evergreens stand out even more against the blandness of the white snow surrounding them. That's how your business can stand out—and thrive—if you heed the advice that follows.

Alan Weiss, Ph.D., author *Million Dollar Consulting*
April 2014

ACKNOWLEDGMENTS

Feel free to start the music (or flip to a commercial) if I drone on too long.

Thanks to my parents, who always pushed me to create my own map and follow my own path. Thanks, Dad, for, as long as I can remember, telling me to write my own paycheck.

Thanks to my grandparents, the late Orville and Vera Fleming, June Farbiak, and especially Grandpa John, for sharing your amazement of life with me.

Thanks to my good friend Troy Loop. Your relentless daily mentorship, feedback, and ideas were invaluable during the writing of this book. Thanks to Shawn Veltman, the second-smartest person I know, for the almost-daily Skype chats, late-night phone calls, and brainstorm sessions. You are a true marketing genius.

Thanks to my literary agent, Esmond Harmsworth, for your wonderful advice, support, and encouragement while I was writing my book proposal and for your careful pursuit of the right publisher for this book. Thanks to the hardworking group at AMACOM, including senior acquisitions editor Bob Nirkind (you believed in this book from day one!), and the incredible design team (your cover design is ingenious!).

Thanks to my editor extraordinaire, Alison Hagge. Your attention to detail, optimism, and encouragement was invaluable.

Thanks to my mentor, Alan Weiss, for always reminding me the ultimate goal of writing a business book is not to be an author, but to help others improve their businesses and enrich their lives.

Thanks to Seth Godin, for dinner in Chicago, where you challenged me to "ship." I still remember the response you wrote to my e-mail where I confessed that I wished that I could write books like you. You said, "If you write a book, I'll read it." Well, here it is, Seth.

Thanks to all my clients for being open to new ideas and trusting in my advice to help your organizations grow. Thanks for following me, and not the herd.

Thanks to my cousin Holly Morin, one of the most talented designers in the world. You transformed my scribbled-on-a-napkin ideas to the effective process visuals found in this book.

Finally, thanks to all my supportive family members, friends, and colleagues: Wes Fleming, Josh Stipancic, Dan Weedin, Roberta Matuson, Jean Oursler, Gary Patterson, Yael Grauer, Andrew Miller, Colleen Francis, Dorie Clark, Shawn Casemore, and Stu McLaren.

Evergreen

Seeing the Forest for the Trees

If you ever get the chance to travel to Vancouver Island in British Columbia, don't miss Cathedral Grove. En route to our final destination, Tofino, a quaint town just on the edge of the Pacific Ocean and as far west as one can go in Canada, my wife, Heather, and I traveled down the bumpy, winding highway in our small rental car and eventually made it to the halfway point.

Cathedral Grove is one of those rare spots on the planet that maintains an almost caricature-like feeling. It's as if you've entered a surreal scene in the latest Pixar film. Nestled within MacMillan Provincial Park, the trees here are old—really old—some almost 800 years old. People from all over the world come to walk these forest trails canopied by ancient, towering Douglas firs, some more than 250 feet high. My wife and I took the obligatory tourist photos of each other trying to wrap our arms around the massive trunks.

We then sat for a while and took in everything as the trees swayed in the wind. I couldn't help but think this isn't the place I'd want to be if a large windstorm came rolling through, but at that moment it was simply peaceful. After walking for a while, we came upon a break in the forest that led to a small stream. We sat down on the water's edge to relax for a few minutes, and though I was on my honeymoon and business should have been the furthest thing from my mind, I couldn't help it. Something about the evergreen trees intrigued me.

Then I realized: A great business is like an evergreen. Over time it, too, can grow to be a giant, towering above others. Its presence in the landscape is often awe-inspiring. It can be steadfast. Short of an act of God, scandal, or major industry disruption, such a business—like an evergreen—can weather most storms. Its customers are analogous to leaves (or perhaps more precisely, needles, since an evergreen is a conifer), and this kind of company is able to build incredible, long-lasting relationships with its customers. Consequently, evergreens remain lush, healthy, and green all year round. By contrast, other companies struggle to keep their customers, or routinely shed them as though they are dead leaves, and therefore are forced to continuously grow new leaves (or add new customers) in order to survive.

The analogy is a simple one, but I've found myself coming back to it again and again. One question in particular really resonates with me:

> *How is it that some companies seem able to effortlessly create customer loyalty (thereby increasing their profits), while others seem to be constantly dropping existing customers and simultaneously struggling to find new ones?*

Over the years I've spent a great deal of time working with companies across a variety of industries, and I'm positioned to answer that question. It has everything to do with the relationship between the company and the customer—how the company approaches that relationship, what systems it puts into place, and how it thinks about marketing. Most companies do not build those relationships beyond lip service—beyond the typical (and tired) assertion, "We provide *wow* service!"

Great companies do more. They spend the time to continually cultivate and nurture relationships with their customers, from even before they were actually customers! When a company invests in this manner, its customer relationships develop and become as strong as they can be, with customer loyalty becoming a key factor of the relationship. Like the roots of an 800-year-old tree, this loyalty eventually becomes capable of supporting tremendous and continuous growth. This is the kind of company that becomes Evergreen.

WHY I WROTE THIS BOOK

When it comes to working with clients, I'm a pragmatist. I want my clients to experience dramatic results, and quickly. My work can be boiled down to helping them answer two simple questions: How do you most effectively get a new customer? And more important: Once you have that customer, how do you keep that customer for life?

My clients have come from all over the world and have worked in hundreds of different industries. However, throughout the past decade, I have largely focused on online entities. I became known in Internet circles as the Customer Retention Guy. I am the person companies call when they want to figure out why they are losing customers, and how to stop the bleeding.

It became apparent that many problems were similar from one company to the next. I soon identified three distinct areas where problems could be located and solutions implemented. I named them the Three Cs of an Evergreen organization. Once I saw these patterns clearly, I could easily solve dozens of problems related to everything from sales and marketing to customer service to employee retention and more. In short, I could help a business go from losing customers and money one day to keeping customers and making money the next. Companies started bringing me in to do consultations, strategy sessions, workshops, and assessments. I worked with marketing departments, sales teams, customer service divisions, senior executives, and CEOs. It was satisfying, to say the least, to recognize that so many complex business challenges could stem from one of these three distinct areas.

But this book isn't about me. This book is about *you* and your business. I'm here to help you now! I make some bold suggestions in the first half of the book. For example, I debunk the myth that companies should spend so much energy (and money) focusing on new customer acquisition, arguing that this is actually the root cause of at least half of their problems. I also introduce and explain the Three Cs of an Evergreen organization—character, community, and content. These are the core principles that I believe generate true customer loyalty—and not just a pie-in-the-sky feeling of loyalty.

In the second half of the book, I make more bold suggestions. For instance, I believe the traditional Four Ps of marketing are dead, and there's actually a far more simplistic way to think about marketing. To change your results you need to reevaluate the paradigm that was true yesterday and exchange it for the paradigm that is true today. Our world has changed. In these chapters I focus on the tactical and customer-retention–enhancing approaches that are available to all businesses. There are discussions about social media strategies, customer loyalty programs (and the types of rewards your customers *really* crave), customer lifetime value (CLV), and the ways that new customers interact with and communicate with your business. I also show you how to deal with customer complaints, when to fire a customer, and how to have new customers fall in love with you.

Note: Throughout the book I most often use the term *customer*, but you can use it interchangeably with *client*. I'm not here to argue the subtle distinctions between these two terms. Call them whatever you prefer, provided it forces you to treat every one of them with deep and profound respect.

The core message of this book is that keeping customers is not a mysterious process. It's not magical. Loyalty isn't some mythical essence that some companies are lucky to have. It's built and created. Plus, it's downright simple to create when you have the right understanding of how all the pieces fit together. *Evergreen: Cultivate the Enduring Customer Loyalty*

That Keeps Your Business Thriving presents timeless principles for keeping customers happy, using frequent examples drawn from both high-profile companies and my own client files to demonstrate these principles in action—and it provides the tools you need to make it easy for you to apply each of these principles.

I'll make you this promise: On the pages that follow, I'll show you what's worked with hundreds of my clients—how we've been able to shift from a pure how-do-we-get-more-new-customers outlook to a how-do-we-better-care-for-our-existing-customers mindset. Each time I've helped my clients make this shift, the results have been impressive. Everything has changed—from referrals, to word-of-mouth, to profit maximization, to marketing effectiveness. Character, community, and content are the roots of any successful company with truly loyal customers. Furthermore, the biggest benefits come to those who are able to apply these concepts long before they win the customer. What I'm presenting here is a system that can be used not only to dramatically grow your business—but also to ensure that your company will survive over the next ten years.

WHO THIS BOOK IS FOR

From service professionals on the front lines to sales professionals, sole proprietors, small and medium-size business owners, senior-level executives, and even Fortune 500 CEOs, anyone whose business sells products, service, or information, and thus has a customer, will learn and benefit from the material in this book. Furthermore, I challenge anyone who has been addicted to a we-need-more-new-customers-now philosophy primarily because it seemed the only way to grow a company. (It isn't. There's a better way. Read on.) I conceived and created this book for you.

Throughout *Evergreen*, I use a variety of stories and examples that touch on a number of different industries. Please remember: *Be open to new ideas.* The marketplace has changed with advances in technology. It is only logical that your approach to marketing should follow suit with this new paradigm. Don't dismiss ideas if you find your business and your customers are different from those discussed. Everyone's customers are different. And yet the concepts that I've used to help small and medium-size businesses are the same as those being used by companies such as Amazon and Apple (and they might not even realize it).

WHY YOU SHOULD READ THIS BOOK

Today's customers demand something unlike anything they have ever wanted in the past—a connection with your business. This means that in order to increase customer loyalty, you need to create a relationship with that customer on a deeper and much more profound level.

I believe that becoming Evergreen requires an entirely new way of thinking about the market, our customers, and our marketing efforts. When we are able to change our thinking and how we represent ourselves (both in the marketplace as well as with our existing customers), we create a better, richer, and more fulfilling experience for the customer. When we, as business owners, take a vested interest in making these changes to our day-to-day operations and, more important, change how we approach relationships between our companies and our customers, we can't help but build authentic customer loyalty.

By following the advice in this book, you will plant a seed that will take root and grow your business like the towering evergreens of Cathedral Grove. You'll be required to think differently, even counterintuitively, about everything you've done in the past with regard to marketing your business, communicating with new and existing customers, approaching social media and using the Web, managing your reputation off-line and online, and dealing with negative feedback and irate customers. I'll show you why the customer is *not* always right, and why not every customer is worth keeping. I'll explain why some customers are worth fighting to bring back, and why sometimes your disloyal customers might offer you the greatest opportunity to increase profits. The content that I'm going to share in this book requires you to be bold, be willing to take a step into the unknown, and be able to accept a level of uncertainty.

Here's what I can tell you with a fair amount of certainty: By implementing what you learn in *Evergreen*, you'll acquire customers faster. You'll also create legitimate brand loyalty—the type of loyalty that leads to customers ranting and raving about your business, that generates massive referrals and strong word-of-mouth, and that isn't swayed by cheaper prices, more features, or (often ineffective) rewards cards. You'll hold on to customers even if your products and services cost more. You'll also reduce your marketing and advertising spending and increase spending on the customers who already do business with you, and they'll return that spending twenty times over. You'll develop a richer, more complex customer experience that resonates with your customer. Finally, you'll no longer wander the social media landscape, wondering if anyone is listening; you'll know exactly where to be, where to go, and what to say.

I could keep going, but I'm going to go out on a limb and suggest that what I've already stated might be enough to keep you interested. This is a book for visionaries—those willing to look at the act of "conducting" business in a different light. Those willing to accept it's not just "business as usual" anymore.

Welcome to Evergreen.

PART ONE

Establishing Roots

CHAPTER 1

Debunking the Myth

New Customers Will Not Save Your Business

In November 2011, Rachel Brown's bakery, Need a Cake, received the kind of attention many people dream of but never expect to actually get. Feature stories were written about her in *The Telegraph* and on the Huffington Post, MSNBC, and BBC websites, among others. It was the kind of publicity that would, in almost all cases, be unattainable for a small shop like hers.

After twenty-five years in business, Brown was in the news because her small bakery had done something phenomenal. She had enticed more than 8,500 new customers to her shop in the blink of an eye. But before I share the details about what happened and how Brown got this influx of new customers, I want to ask you a very simple question: Is it really a good thing for a business, of any size, to get 8,500 new customers practically overnight?

Before you answer, let me ask another question: When you hear Brown's story, are you thinking about the amount of additional revenue your business could receive if you were able to attract 8,500 new customers? Are you envisioning those empty parts of the day when you find yourself wondering whether anyone might actually walk through the door? If this sounds familiar, you're not alone. Most people—especially small-business owners—think just that. Of course, larger organizations can learn from this story, too, which is my intent.

In this chapter, I'm going to take on the myth that new customers will save your business. It's a myth that businesses, both large and small, believe wholeheartedly. On the pages that follow, I will demonstrate that new customers are, in fact, a mixed blessing and, further, that putting all your energy into the pursuit of new customers can actually destroy your business. I'm not saying that new customers are inherently bad. Of course not. Obviously, every business needs new customers to grow and thrive. But in almost every case in every company, focusing on getting them takes a tremendous amount of time, effort, energy, and money away from areas where it would be much better spent—like developing deeper relationships with your existing customer base.

The theme of this chapter is simple. If you had the choice, would you want to bring in 100 new customers and watch 50 (or even more) of them run away, never to return again? Or would you rather make a few simple changes to ensure you are consistently strengthening your business relationships with your existing customer base, while also putting new structures in place to make your business entirely Evergreen, where new customers can both flourish and grow with your organization, bringing long-term and perpetual profits? The choice should be obvious.

THE ALLURE OF NEW BUSINESS CAN BE FATAL

Let's get back to Rachel Brown and her gourmet cake shop, which she owned and operated in Reading, England. Business was good, but business can always be better. She'd heard of this new website called Groupon, where she could offer potential "new customers" a discount to try her service. Groupon offered her a flood of new business—and the company certainly lived up to its promise.[1]

If you are not familiar with Groupon, here's how it works: A company will offer a significant discount off its products or services—sometimes as high as 75 percent. Customers then purchase the discounted coupon (called a Groupon). The customer wins by scoring a great discount at a local business. Groupon wins by taking its cut (a percentage of what's left after the discount—usually another 50 percent). Finally, the business "wins" by attracting new customers. (In reality, though, the business is paid whatever is left over, plus credit card processing fees. In other words, for every $100 Groupon, the business might receive fewer than $25 after all is said and done.)

Brown's promotion worked—a little too well. She was swamped. In fact, she suddenly found herself inundated with more than 8,500 new customers! She had to hire emergency staff to handle the orders that were coming in, but they had barely a fraction of the training and experience of her regular employees. All of this led to a drop in the quality of her product and the quality of her service. Those new customers likely didn't walk away from the experience telling their friends about the best red velvet cupcake they'd ever eaten at Need a Cake. Instead, they probably said something like, "I stood in line for so long to get *this*!"

Many fatal business mistakes can be traced directly back to a company's focus on acquiring new customers, its lack of appreciation of existing customers, or its lack of understanding customers' wants and needs. Unfortunately, in Brown's case, the misstep wiped out nearly a year's worth of profits and left her deeply regretting her decision. Brown later said, "Without a doubt, it was the worst business decision I ever made."[2]

To be fair to Brown, her worst business decision ever wasn't entirely her fault. The horror stories of companies, especially small ones, sideswiped by the allure of new customers are all too common. Groupon, for example, can be an absolutely wonderful customer acquisition tool for many businesses. But for all the brilliance and effectiveness Groupon brings to getting new customers through its clients' doors, it is monumentally bad at helping those businesses keep their new customers—an area where I believe Groupon has dramatically underserved its client base.[3]

WE'RE ALL ADDICTED TO SEX—
AND WHAT THAT MEANS FOR YOUR BUSINESS

To understand what really went wrong with Brown's business, we need to first understand, on a deeper level, why businesses are so focused on *getting* customers and not on *keeping* customers. It's easy to understand the draw for a small business. As the late management guru Peter Drucker often said, "Without customers, there is no business." Customers are the lifeblood of any business, and for a small business the allure of the new customer is sometimes too great.

Let me share with you a story about an experience I had with my own bank. I had applied for a commercial line of credit for my consulting company and was promised everything would be completed within forty-eight hours. Nearly two months later, my line of credit was finally completed. When I asked the manager why it took so long, he said flat out, "Honestly, Noah, we're so busy with new customers that we don't have the time and resources to devote to our existing customers." Before you scream and pull your hair out, recognize that the manager simply told me what many organizations, including perhaps your own, are going through at this very moment. The reason: We're all addicted to sex.

Let me explain. In 2012, I presented the closing keynote address to more than 400 publishing executives at their annual conference in Washington, D.C. I began the lunchtime talk with a slide that read, "We're all addicted to sex!" The clanging of knives and forks went silent as I watched people scramble to find their notebooks, open their laptops, or clean up the water they had just spilled on themselves.

I didn't plan to start this way, but I had just spent three days sitting in on various sessions at the conference and listening to other speakers. Three out of every four presentations were focused on split testing different text colors and fonts in e-mails (HTML or plain text, size 12 or 14 headlines) as well as optimal sending times (Tuesdays or Wednesdays) and other assorted minutiae of marketing campaigns. The companies presenting this data had certainly done some innovative and creative testing, but it was extremely worrisome to me to see how many businesses, large and small, online and off-line, were more enamored with trying to determine whether it was better to send an e-mail at 9:30 a.m. or 10:26 a.m. than they were with ensuring that the e-mail had something interesting or relevant to say.

The Thrill of the Chase

In the marketing world, retention is boring and optimization (especially around acquiring new customers) is sexy. It feels great, and you get practically immediate feedback on how good your marketing is and if it's working—very similar to, well, sex. When a large organization steps up to the plate and spends big bucks to run something like a Super Bowl advertisement, it's pretty simple to measure results almost immediately after the campaign runs. Websites crash, customers tweet, fans like the Facebook page, and sales increase. It often provides instant gratification, and it feels good—again, very similar to, well, sex.

No question about it, the ability to stimulate immediate sales is sexy. But I'm not convinced it is doing us any good in the long run—especially when those same organizations aren't focused on keeping the customers they just spent Fort Knox to get. I work diligently with all my clients to keep them from getting so wrapped up in their sex addiction that they forget to love their customers. Immediate marketing results—like impressions, conversions, traffic, sales, e-mail open rates, and new subscribers—is all really attractive stuff. The thrill of the chase. The satisfaction of the successful seduction. I get it. But it's got nothing on long-term customer retention, which is more analogous to love. Love involves having a relationship with your customers, it survives long past the initial glitz and glamour of that first encounter, and it's ultimately far more fulfilling for both parties.

The Power of an Alternate Mindset

There's an old analogy in the business world—the Leaky Bucket Theory. This analogy suggests that most businesses operate like a leaky bucket.

The idea is that your business is the bucket and the water in your bucket represents your customers. The holes in the bucket are the various areas where you lose your customers. Most businesses tend to focus on adding more water instead of simply fixing the holes. But I digress. We don't have leaky buckets. We have deciduous trees. Deciduous companies like to invest heavily in marketing, and, more often than not, their marketing works.

My bank was busy. Banks have no problem putting new leaves on the tree. They are swamped with new customers, but like those on a deciduous tree, these leaves stayed temporarily, because as soon as banks close the deal, they move on to bigger and better things—the "more exciting" new customers. My bank was willing to lose me, a loyal, long-time customer with a considerable amount of future value to the organization, because it was too busy focusing on new customers. Instead of banking on an asset, it was gambling with its reserves—no pun intended. Many organizations don't realize that this mindset is costing them millions and millions of dollars. They fail to recognize the true costs of a new customer focus, such as the additional time, effort, energy, and money required to persuade these customers to buy from them in the first place, and the opportunity costs associated with trying to appeal to these new customers.

My client experience has demonstrated that when an organization can truly understand, and integrate, the relationship between its profit, growth, longevity, customer relationships, employee empowerment, and customer service, then real, impactful, tectonic shifts are generated on its financial statements. This is also the single best way to ensure a business can become Evergreen. Let me say that again:

> *If you want to experience dramatic growth within your organization, you must truly understand the relationship between profit, growth, longevity, customer relationships, employee empowerment, and customer service.*

The cost of ongoing customer engagement is nothing compared with the cost of acquiring new customers.

THE LATEST BOARDROOM BUZZWORD:
CUSTOMER-CENTRICITY

I'm sure you've heard about the concepts of "customer-centricity" and "big data," especially if you work in a large organization or read the business section of *The New York Times*. The problem is that most people use these terms without truly understanding them. I'm bothered by the many organizations that claim to be customer-centric on paper but haven't internalized the concepts or truly put customer-focused initiatives into action. I can't state it much better than management consultant and author Jay Galbraith, who wrote that a majority of companies claim to be customer-centric with nothing more than a "cosmetic gloss of customer focus sprinkled around the edges."[4] My goal as a consultant is to help companies go beyond a cosmetic gloss. I'm more interested in your organization getting a permanent tattoo of customer focus. When you are tattooed with a message, you've internalized it and there's no turning back.

What Does It Mean to Be Customer-Centric?

The term *customer-centric* has been getting a lot of attention lately in the business world, though, as with many business buzzwords, everybody seems to have his or her own definition. In a 2010 article in the *Harvard Business Review*, Harvard professor Ranjay Gulati defines it as "looking at an enterprise from the outside-in rather than the inside-out—that is, through the lens of the customer rather than the producer."[5]

Wharton professor Peter Fader uses this definition: Customer-centricity is "a strategy that aligns a company's development and delivery of its products and services with the current and future needs of a select set of customers in order to maximize their long-term financial value to the firm."[6]

Actually, the ideas behind customer-centricity go back a long time. More than fifty years ago, Peter Drucker was talking about customer-centricity when he made statements like, "A company's primary responsibility is to serve its customers. Profit is not the primary goal, but rather an essential condition for the company's continued existence. There is only one valid definition of business purpose: to create a customer."[7]

You'll find Drucker's books inside almost any executive's office. Have those executives simply failed to grasp the true meaning of his words? Or is the constant pursuit of new customers with disregard to existing customers a simpler, more exciting ambition for companies? As customer-centricity takes a prominent seat in boardrooms everywhere, I believe we need to get clear on this.

What Will a Customer-Centric Mindset Do for *Your* Business?

We are living in a new era of how business is conducted. In fact, this is a profoundly revolutionary time to be operating a business. Our customers are more knowledgeable than ever before. Not only that, they have gained the upper hand in their ability to exert, expect, and demand the way they'll do business and with whom. For an organization to survive it needs to think about its customers and their experiences in an entirely new way. So what's next?

We need to dig a deeper hole for our Evergreens—to ensure our root systems have the room they need to spread and grow. That's what's next. This is why the concept of customer-centricity is so important. In Fader's definition, customer-centricity is really about customer selection—identifying the most profitable group of customers and focusing attention and resources on them to encourage greater participation, retention, and ultimately profitability. Today, we know more about our customers than ever before. But knowing more or using fancy phrases at our strategy sessions means nothing if we're not able to use that knowledge wisely.

You've probably all heard of the 80/20 rule, also known as the Pareto principle. It states that for many events, roughly 80 percent of the effects come from 20 percent of the causes. In my consulting work, I've found that the 80/20 rule remains true in almost every business, of every size, regardless of industry. The top 20 percent of customers generate 80 percent of profits. Our mistake, however, is that we are not spending enough time or resources on the top 20 percent. Remember, just having access to a lot of data and claiming to be customer-centric doesn't mean you are truly focused on what's best for the customer.

THE TRUE VALUE OF A CUSTOMER

What's a customer really worth? Now, this is a tough question—one that many organizations struggle to answer properly, but it is certainly an important one to discuss. Later in the book I'll bring you back to planet earth and make a few commonsense, on-the-ground suggestions, but for now, let's explore how most larger organizations determine the value of a customer and expose a number of misconceptions tied to the way it's currently done.

Understanding the Limitations of the Customer Lifetime Value (CLV) Model

Most organizations focus on measuring customer lifetime value, sometimes referred to as average customer lifetime value. CLV is often seen as the Holy Grail of data analysis. It's an idea that's seductively simple and makes great intuitive sense. It's the reason credit card companies will spend a tremendous amount of money to acquire new customers. They know, with some certainty, what the average customer is worth to them. There are, however, a number of drawbacks to basing a customer's worth on the CLV model.

One major issue has to do with the idea of averages. The reason that keeping customers can be difficult for companies is directly due, in large part, to their practice of viewing their customer base as this single, amorphous blob that can be understood with simple averages: "Our average customer is 37.34 years old, has 1.38 children, a salary of $53,332, and lives in a city of 100,000 people or more. This customer is expected to spend $237.12 with us this year, but let's see if we can get a little bit more with some clever social media marketing!" I'm oversimplifying and dramatizing here, of course, but in looking at the bulk of communications between companies and their customers, can there be any doubt that most companies are far less interested in you as an individual than in you as part of "their customer base"?

Step out of your role as a business-minded professional for a minute and into the role of a consumer, which you are as well. Think about your own interactions with various companies: When was the last time you got an e-mail, an auto-responder, or a canned response? Think about the last time you called a customer support line. More to my point, think about the last time you were treated as "average." How did that make you feel? I very much doubt you are seeing visions of sugarplums!

Here's the other major issue with CLV. If you just look at the customer lifetime value, which is an average across an entire customer base, you can't determine the commonalities among those customers who stopped doing business with you early on, in order to address why they left. Nor can you identify the commonalities among customers who continue doing business with you year after year, in order to encourage new customers to follow the same path. Have you ever tried to do this? If so, does it feel as though you are just throwing darts?

Using CLV Data Creatively

Looking only at a single CLV number clouds a lot of useful information. As an example, consider a small to medium-size business that spends $50,000 per year on each of its two primary channels of new customers: Google Pay-Per-Click (PPC) ads and good old-fashioned referrals. With a firm grasp on the average CLV, this company may believe that as long as it is putting enough leaves on the tree, everything will be just dandy.

But it might be the case that only 10 percent of referrals end their relationship with the company within the first forty-five days, while 60 percent of PPC customers quit during the same time frame. Knowing this, the company's managers might decide to dramatically reduce spending on PPCs and increase spending on referral generation. Of course, they *don't* know—because they're using a single number to make important marketing decisions.

There are ways to make customer lifetime value more useful, including finding multiple CLVs across different segmentations of a customer base. For example:

- What's the customer lifetime value of males under age 30?

- How about females over age 40?

- What about customers who made their first purchase of greater than $100 within the first week?

- What's the total CLV of all customers vs. the CLV of customers with more than ten purchases?

- What's the CLV of customers who used a coupon or took advantage of a sale on their first visit vs. the total CLV?

Once we begin to look at subsets, we enter into the territory of data modeling, which brings us straight to this "big data" thing you keep hearing about. Does your head hurt yet? I know mine does.

Recognizing the Truth About "Big Data"

In a nutshell, here's the truth about big data: It's not size that matters; it's how you use it. Seriously! Organizations have more data than ever before. We know more about our customers than we ever thought possible, and we're beginning to use that data to make some insightful decisions. Some exceptionally customer-centric organizations are making great strides in this regard, using that data to make a more positive experience for their customers.

Amazon, for example, is one of the most customer-centric companies of our time. Some people would argue it is the most customer-centric company on the planet. Amazon is one of my favorite examples of an Evergreen organization. From early on, it focused with laserlike precision on the customer and the customer's experience. It continues to push the envelope by learning more about its customers and tailoring the experience to them. I'm sure you've shopped on Amazon. What happens is that while you're looking for products, Amazon's systems are helping products find you. It can be scary and daunting to realize that Amazon knows more about your shopping habits than your own spouse does.

Personal privacy and creepiness factors of big data collection aside, I love telling the story of how Kmart knew a teenage girl was pregnant before her own father did based on how her purchasing patterns matched the company's models of the purchases of pregnant women. On the other end of the spectrum, the magic of all this data is that it enables companies to be more responsive in not only meeting but also exceeding their customers' expectations. It allows organizations to create and tailor ongoing conversations with their customers.

Putting Your Equity Where It Matters

When it comes to the various ways of using big data, it's easy to fall down the rabbit hole. Of course, I fully expect large organizations to continue to improve upon their usage of CLV calculations, but for the sake of this book, I'd like to make a few simpler suggestions.[8] Your customer base is the single most valuable asset your business has. Not your employees. Not your products or services. Your customers. As noted earlier in the Peter Drucker quote, "Without customers, there is no business."

The value of that asset is determined by a number of things, but primarily it is based on the equity you build into the customer relationship and the future value you can derive from that asset. It doesn't get simpler than that. Big data is important—but only if we use it to support our customers' needs. We need to start making smart decisions about our investments. When we view everything as an "average," we often make important business decisions based on only half-good information.

If you were a real estate investor, for example, you wouldn't buy a dumpy home in a dumpy neighborhood with little future potential. You would look for an investment property with decent current value and lots of potential value. On the other hand, you might look for something with a low current value but the potential for a big future payoff. Just like investing in the stock market, a smart, balanced investment portfolio contains a mix of low-risk investments alongside riskier investments. But why do companies insist on investing almost everything on new customers? These investments have no history. This is seriously risky business. Our customers are not all created equal. Do you believe your marketing dollars are generating their maximum return when you invest equally in all your customers? No.

It quickly becomes obvious that knowing *how* to use the data to increase the value of a customer, or a group of customers, is much more important than simply acquiring piles and piles of data. Furthermore, if we really want to increase the value of our customers through the use of our data, then the most important kind of data we can collect is behavioral. When a school of fish swims together, all the fish face in the same direction. If a single fish turns, for whatever reason—it might see the shadow of a wading fly fisherman or catch the scent of a tasty morsel, for instance—the other fish often turn as well. They act in unison. Customers act in a similar fashion.

Applying These Concepts to Your Business

Whenever I work with online entities like subscription and paywall sites, I typically show them how to precisely monitor, measure, and track consumption, usage, and participation data of their customers, and how to sort those customers into groups based on their likelihood of future profitability, with each group requiring its own marketing, contact, and communication plans to ensure they receive the most value from the company. Make sense? Any business can apply these techniques, including yours. Just remember: Your primary goal must be to make wise decisions about where to invest your dollars with the highest potential for future value.

As we've compiled massive amounts of data, we are in a much stronger position than we've been in the past, which means we are less dependent on guessing. There's a good chance you have an incredibly talented team of marketers and engineers sifting through your customer data. And if you don't, I'll show you how small, family-owned businesses have used these concepts on a small scale with massive impact. The rest is really about using a commonsense approach to tie it all together. When you do that, you can make wise decisions about the path your customer travels when conducting business with your organization, and you strengthen both the relationship and conversation between customer and company, never letting that customer stray too far off the path.

Further on in the book, I'll demonstrate how easy it is to set up *Mission: Impossible*–style alarms that let the appropriate management or customer care staff know when your customers' usage patterns indicate that there is a high risk of losing them, and know how to enable personalized contact (or, alternatively, how to set up systems that recognize these patterns and automatically take the appropriate action). Remember that school of fish—when one fish turns, they all turn. I'll show you how to recognize when this might be happening, and what you can do to stop it.

INTRODUCING THE EVERGREEN
MARKETING EQUILIBRIUM

A few years ago, I met with a client whose marketing team was solely focused on "getting" more new customers, while paying almost zero attention to "keeping" existing customers. This client didn't have a leaky bucket; he had a bottomless bucket! More appropriate to our broader

Evergreen analogy, though, his business was like a shriveled-up tree without any leaves and with a rotting root system, yet the gardener insisted that he keep watering it.

This client kept talking about his team's impressive "sales closing" ratios. Perhaps he had been overly inspired by Alec Baldwin's classic "Always Be Closing" speech in the film *Glengarry Glen Ross*. However, I don't believe you "close" a sale—you "open" a relationship.

The sales transaction is the start of the relationship, not the end. Sales professionals everywhere would instantly become better at what they do if they simply banished the idea of "closing." This client in particular was leaving millions of dollars on the table by hyperfocusing on the sales closings.

The Evergreen Marketing Equilibrium, shown in Figure 1-1, represents the balance between customer acquisition and customer retention that an Evergreen business must maintain in order to stay healthy. Bal-

FIGURE 1-1

The Evergreen Marketing Equilibrium

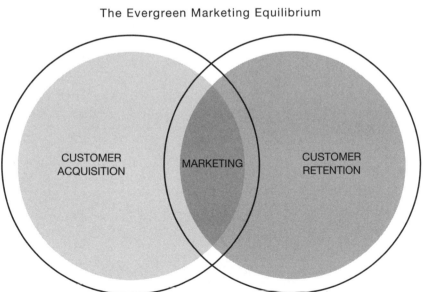

ance represents stability in your marketing efforts. I created this visual on the spot while talking with my "bottomless bucket" client.

When comparing my client's operations with the Evergreen Marketing Equilibrium, we concluded that because his customer acquisition and customer retention efforts were two entirely separate processes, the circles weren't touching. His sole focus was getting new customers, which meant that his marketing efforts were completely out of whack. Figure 1-2 shows what was happening in his operations: He brought in new customers (indicated by the arrows), but most just slipped out the bottom. Through happenstance (and not any deliberate marketing efforts) a few of these customers stayed on, and they moved over to the retention circle. Without proper balance between customer acquisition and customer retention, it's difficult to market your business effectively. In this situation, gravity seems to have a stronger pull than any "marketing" that's being done. Unfortunately, Figure 1-2 depicts the situation many organizations are in.

FIGURE 1-2

Unsustainable Marketing Scenario

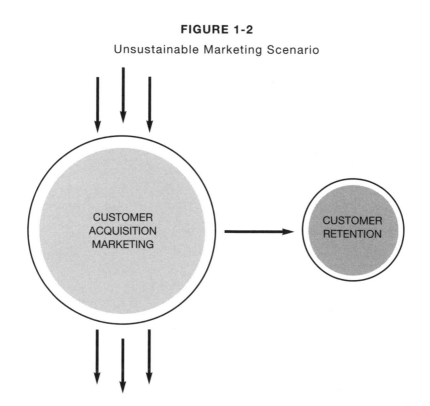

The Evergreen Marketing Equilibrium is a surprisingly simple concept, but it's worth asking yourself: How would you diagram *your* organization's marketing efforts? Since an equilibrium is the balance of two opposing forces, you obviously want to treat them as one. But as a Customer Retention Guy, I tend to focus on adding even more weight to the right-hand side. A little bit of instability is okay, as long as you are more focused on how you're going to keep the customers once you have them.

Let's consider what this all means. If your circles aren't touching, chances are you have:

- Low marketing effectiveness

- High customer acquisition costs

- High churn

- High stress

If you are able to balance the Evergreen Marketing Equilibrium in your business, you'll experience:

- Higher marketing effectiveness

- Enhanced customer loyalty

- Lower customer acquisition costs

- Less customer attrition

- Increased profits

- Better understanding of your customers

- More referrals

- Greater word-of-mouth

- More valuable customers

- Greater success

The Evergreen Marketing Equilibrium provokes thought, doesn't it? It is challenging because it hits home for many organizations. Growth is good. New customers are a necessity. Nobody would argue against that. But most organizations don't understand the true cost of a narrow-minded focus on acquiring new customers.

When we look even deeper into the true cost of lost time, we find an enormous profit killer. This time would be much better spent deepening relationships with existing customers—and the results would be far more fruitful than any customer acquisition escapades could ever offer. I guarantee it. Focusing solely on acquisition (in hopes that you can stop the leaves from dropping, or so that you can continue to add new leaves, as needed) is a wasteful, myopic, and arrogant business strategy—one that is followed and embraced all too often.

This is really the essence of Evergreen. I'm talking to companies all the time that are looking for something more. They are looking to improve conversions. They are looking to write better ad copy and create viral videos. They are figuring out the best time of day to send an e-mail or post to their blog. They're collecting more data. And all this is happening while their current customers continue to drop like dead leaves.

It doesn't have to be that way.

CHAPTER **2**

Surveying the Landscape

The Essential Components
of an Evergreen Organization

GoldieBlox is sweeping the nation. The Super Bowl XLVIII commercial provocatively introduced the company (which has a unique line of girl-focused building toys) to a mass audience in 2014. The ad shows girls using pulleys to lower a pink unicorn "rocking horse" from a second-story balcony, girls loading a pink princess fort onto a makeshift cargo freighter fashioned out of skateboards, and girls pedaling an elaborate contraption fastened to a pink tricycle down a street—this blur of pink snowballs, earnestly and at breakneck speed. Boys, befuddled, leap out of the way of this increasingly boisterous group. Hundreds of girls charge their final destination—a beauty pageant taking place at the park. Beneath an archway of pink balloons, young female pageant participants seem relieved by the invasion, greeting them enthusiastically and then shedding their tiaras. From here, a cascade of the pink toys are loaded onto a pink rocket ship and blown off to space.

The ad is set to the classic rock song "Cum On Feel the Noize" by Quiet Riot. The ad replaces the lyrics with girls chanting, "Come on, ditch your toys. Girls make some noise. More than pink, pink, pink, we want to *THINK!*" Needless to say, the ad has gone viral.

GoldieBlox is the brainchild of Debbie Sterling, a Stanford-educated engineer who is now the company's CEO. When Sterling began college she quickly realized that there weren't many other women in her program. She wondered if it might be because other women her age were given the same toys she received as a child—dolls, doll houses, and lots and lots of cute (but less-than-purposeful) pink *stuff*. In those days (and it wasn't so long ago—Sterling is only in her thirties now), toys for building and tinkering weren't made for girls. They were only for boys. In the intervening years, manufacturers of classic kids' building toys, such as Lincoln Logs, have "feminized" their product lines by simply adding a pink roof here or pink packaging there.

Sterling decided to change things, and she set out to make the activity of building appeal on a more fundamental level to young girls. During her extensive research phase, she realized that while girls naturally enjoy building, they typically also love to read. In a stroke of genius, she decided to combine the two activities. When girls play with GoldieBlox, they read a story about Goldie and follow along, using gears, pulleys, levers, strings, and other tools to help her build solutions to specific problems she encounters. Pure brilliance! Consequently, Sterling's company has captured the hearts and minds of millions of girls everywhere. More relevant to our discussion, however, she beautifully implements everything I'm going to teach you in the next three chapters—almost to a tee. And chances are, Sterling herself probably does not even realize that her company embodies the Three Cs.

In the three chapters that follow, I will present a new method for creating long-lasting relationships with your customers and much more effective marketing. It's a strategic framework that you can use to help your company or organization become Evergreen. This new approach will allow you to better understand customer retention, reduce customer attrition, and enhance the customer experience and customer loyalty. I call this strategic framework the Three Cs of an Evergreen organization.

INTRODUCING THE THREE Cs

For an organization to thrive and move forward in our rapidly changing economy, it must embrace the Three Cs: character, community, and content. By carefully considering each of the Three Cs, and thinking about how these ideas relate to your own company, you will be better positioned to maximize your most important business asset—your customers. You will also naturally develop better ways both to communicate with them and to strengthen your relationships with them.

I had never heard of GoldieBlox until my good friend, the strategic marketing wizard Shawn Veltman (who is familiar with the Three Cs concept), called me one day and said I had to look into this company and what they were doing. "Noah," he said, "this company has *incredible* character, community, and content!"

Shawn was right. GoldieBlox has the perfect combination. It has a unique character (one that is tremendously appealing to mothers and daughters, in particular), a strong customer community (where children participate by uploading videos of their favorite solutions to Goldie's challenges), and incredible content—content that transcends being just a toy and provides incredible value and a dynamic customer experience. It is an inspiring business model.

I'm going to show you a new way to think about approaching *your* business, *your* customers, and *your* marketing. I'm going to show you how to create a company that builds long-lasting customer loyalty through everything you do. This is the game changer that can put your company on a new trajectory unlike any other.

The coming passages serve as introductions to each of the Three C principles. These concepts—and how to apply them to your own business—will be explored in great detail in the three chapters that follow. Stay with me; this is going to be one *fantastic* hike through the Evergreen forest.

The Principle of Character

Character is the first thing that comes to customers' minds when they think about your business. It's analogous to a person. It's your brand personality. It's the "who" your customers think you are.

In their classic book, *Positioning: The Battle for Your Mind*, published more than thirty years ago, Al Ries and Jack Trout demonstrate that most people can remember only a few things about any given company. When companies (and their brands) try to communicate with a customer they compete with millions of other messages. Those messages create a cacophony that makes it difficult for any single company (or brand) to have anything resonate or stick with either current or prospective customers. You think the noise was bad thirty years ago? Today, it is positively deafening. The main takeaway from Ries and Trout's book is that organizations can either decide what those few things will be, or they can let the market decide. Incredibly, most organizations choose the latter.

As you probably guessed, I staunchly advocate for bucking *that* trend. The principle of character is about defining, crafting, and presenting the character traits that you want customers to associate with your organization. Character isn't just another fancy way of marketing to your customers. It's about developing an organizational mindset that articulates why you do what you do, and how to communicate your values more effectively to your customers. Much has been written over the years about brand personality. Most authors, however, don't explain why brand personality is more important than ever for creating customer loyalty, and how to strategically and tactically build your company's character. We will explore these concepts at length in Chapter 3.

The Principle of Community

In May 2012, Warren Buffett spent $142 million to acquire the majority interest in Media General, which at that time published sixty-three daily and weekly newspapers through the southeastern United States. As part of the deal, he announced that he would also loan the company an additional $400 million. Media critics were incredulous. One opinion columnist wrote a blog with the headline "Is He Nuts?"[1] Why would Buffett invest in an industry that had seen such tremendous decline during the previous ten years? Well, as he noted to a gathering of Berkshire Hathaway shareholders, "I think there is a future for newspapers that exist in an area where there is a sense of community."[2]

What Buffett recognized is the often-underappreciated power of the humble local newspaper, the kind of paper that treats the vandalism of a Main Street shop with the same level of gravitas that larger, more globally oriented newspapers give to riots during an international relations summit. These local papers exist, in the words of Hoover Adams, founder of *The Daily Record of Dunn*, North Carolina, one of the most prominent small-town newspapers ever, "for local names and local pictures."[3] Local newspapers have power because they reinforce a sense of community. When people see their neighbors' names, they feel the slight thrill while thinking, *I know him!* When they see their own names, they get excited, knowing that everybody else in town will see their names in print. These are the types of things that strengthen communities, and they are exactly why Buffett recognized that these papers still had value. As Hoover Adams said, "In this day and time, in a small town, everybody knows everybody, and they like to read about everybody."[4]

Robert D. Putnam's wonderful book *Bowling Alone: The Collapse and Revival of American Community*, published in 2000, was one of the first to point out something that many people have felt for decades—that the Western world is losing many of its traditional communities. The central finding of Putnam's research is that participation in any number of social organizations has undergone a major decline, even as individual participation in some of those same activities has dramatically increased. (Membership in bowling leagues, for example, has decreased, while attendance at bowling lanes is higher than ever.) What does this have to do with building customer loyalty for your business? The answer lies in a truth that has become somewhat of a cliché:

> No man is an island, entire of itself; every man is a piece of the continent, a part of the main.[5]

Human beings, by nature, are prone to seek out others who share similar interests, values, and beliefs. People are attracted to brand communities because they help them find others who enjoy the same products and services, or the utility those products and services provide.

In *The Righteous Mind: Why Good People Are Divided by Politics and Religion*, social psychologist Jonathan Haidt draws heavily on the importance of community in our evolutionary history. It was not simply being the fastest, strongest, or most aggressive creature that led to the dramatic rise in the human population over the past 100,000 years, Haidt argues, and it's hard to disagree with him. We are slow, weak, and have few natural weapons. But our ability to work in harmony with others—whether while hunting, building, or defending territory—sets humans apart and allows us to thrive.

The Internet and the rise of mobile communications have both connected and disconnected us. It's easy to feel alone today. That's why when we find groups of people who are like us, we want to become or remain a part of that group. Now here's the most important point: Companies that recognize this need for connection and create structures that allow communities to form have a significant advantage when it comes to retaining customers, building customer loyalty, and maximizing customer value. Chapter 4 is dedicated to showing you how to create a sense of community for and among your customers.

The Principle of Content

Let's round back and talk about GoldieBlox one last time. When Sterling created the company, she didn't simply want to introduce another toy in the marketplace. In fact, the actual product was really secondary to her broader goal. Sterling was on a mission to change the big picture and, in particular, how girls are made to feel in the toy department. Her mission was strengthened by her desire to create an emotionally charged customer experience, one that would impassion girls and their mothers to see the world in a new light.

In the fall of 2012 Sterling sought to raise $150,000 on the popular crowdfunding website Kickstarter to create GoldieBlox and launch it worldwide. She met her initial goal in four days, and when she was done, she had raised more than $285,000 with funds from more than 5,500 individual contributors. The product didn't even exist yet. The only things that existed were a vision and a story. The marketing, word-of-mouth, and passion sold the product before the first drop of plastic was injected into the molds. Now, only a couple of years later, the product can be found in almost every major toy store.

If you read reviews about the actual, physical manifestation of the product, you'll see many that aren't entirely favorable. One reviewer wrote, "Poorly made—I don't know if this is a Q.C. [quality control] problem (it's made in China) or just a bad design. The figures that you put on top of the yellow wheels do not fit snugly, so with the force of turning the wheels, they always fall off unless you pull the ribbon very carefully and slowly.... It's *not* a Lego alternative."[6] Obviously, the quality-control issues should be addressed, but GoldieBlox has already swept the nation with the type of buzz you can't create without strong character and a story that both fascinates and spreads like a wildfire. Sure, some customers have purchased the product just because of the hype, and they might not be in for the long haul. Complaints about the small stuff, like the quality of the plastic, indicate that a particular customer hasn't made an emotional connection with the company that transcends the content. However, loyal customers—those who are enchanted by the character and community—will typically brush off a bad content experience, or an experience that wasn't up to par, simply as an anomaly.

At the most basic level, content is the core of your business. It is a shorthand term I use to describe what your customers are buying from you. In some cases it means products; in others services; and in still others, it's information. Content is the core "thing" the customer receives in exchange for money. It's also the final element of the Three Cs. For a lawyer, the base-level content is advice and the handling of legal matters; for an airline, it's getting a passenger from point A to point B; for a web service, it's the utility of the product. In Sterling's case, it was the actual GoldieBlox toy.

Here's the thing about content: Content is a necessary but insufficient condition for a successful business. Without content, there is no business, but just having fabulous content alone is no guarantee of success. Consider GoldieBlox: The product, what Sterling delivers, is actually secondary to the rest of the equation—the character and community of her company. That said, what she delivers is still immensely important.

We're all engaged in providing something to our customers. The challenge is helping you understand that *what* you provide is actually secondary to *how* you do it, and the experience and feeling it creates within your customers. In Chapter 5 I'll continue this discussion of content and show you how to position your products and services in a way that creates a sense of value on an unprecedented level, in ways you never thought possible.

ORCHESTRATING THE THREE Cs, SO THEY PLAY IN HARMONY

The power of the Three Cs comes from an organizationwide understanding of how they harmoniously work together. Here's the thing: If you want to be Evergreen, you need all three principles to be working together. When they do, your business will change tremendously—and for the better. When they don't, you might not be able to put your finger on it, but something won't feel quite right.

To thrive during the next decade, which promises to be tumultuous and ever-changing, your business must carefully consider all of the Three Cs. Take a look at Figure 2-1.

FIGURE 2-1

The Three Cs in Harmony

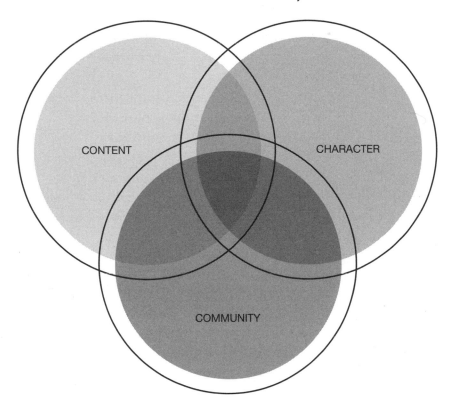

If you have content and community but no character, your company may be perceived as narcissistic, unattractive, and untrustworthy. You have the goods—the products, the services, or the information—but customers recognize that something feels a bit off, they'll never be emotionally attached to the community, even if you have strong community structures in place. You'll create a place for people to vent their concerns but not sing your praises.

If you have content and character but no community, your company may seem like a relic of the 1980s. You come across as though you believe things will eventually return to the way they used to be, and that developments such as the Web and mobile are merely fleeting trends. *A website? Who needs one of those? Facebook? That'll pass.* Customers probably do business with you because of nostalgia, simplicity, or lack of other alternatives. You have a great opportunity! Get used to the world we're living in and embrace this wonderful opportunity to connect and engage with your customers like never before.

If you have community and character but poor content, your company is an empty suit. You have great brand personality and the structures in place to facilitate community, but your products and services are typically perceived by customers to be a letdown. Companies like this can succeed transactionally, but this is a challenging place from which to create organizational growth and increase customer loyalty. Your content must always be top-notch. You must continuously provide value, as well as a sense of excitement for the customer.

If you have great content, great character, and great community, you are poised to build strong customer loyalty and Evergreen relationships. This is the "secret sauce." The Mecca of customer loyalty. This is the recipe used by the most successful companies on the planet. They understand why they do what they do and are able to pass that feeling on to their customers in a way that resonates and creates a genuine emotional impact. They provide the best-quality products or services in the world and pride themselves on both meeting and exceeding the expectations they've set for their customers. Finally, they've put the appropriate systems in place to allow their customers to connect with one another.

Sometimes the community doesn't even have to be pronounced. Take, for example, the classic Apple commercials from the early 2000s that showed black silhouetted bodies dancing while wearing iconic white earbuds and dangling cables. Apple used this ad as a symbol of those in its community. Passing another person with the same white earbuds while swimming in a sea of pedestrians on a New York sidewalk served as a psychic handshake, an acknowledgment between two strangers they were part of the same club.

Imagine what would happen if you could create that type of feeling among your customers. You *can*, and you *will*, and I'm here to show you how.

CHAPTER 3

Examining the Principle
of Character

The Botany of Your Company

Approximately 17 million people visit Amazon.com's website every day.[1] On May 10, 2012, visitors experienced something unexpected. Unlike most other days, when the Amazon home page contains shopping recommendations based on a customer's browsing and purchasing habits or the latest bestselling books, on this day it displayed a handwritten letter on a parchment scroll. It almost looked as if the home page had been taken over by a group of cyberhackers. But it hadn't been hacked. Amazon's CEO, Jeff Bezos, had written it.

"Dear Muggles!" the letter began. Bezos was announcing to Kindle owners, Amazon shoppers, and Harry Potter fans everywhere that the Harry Potter series of books, in e-book format, would soon be available for free in the Kindle Owners' Lending Library. Some might call it cutesy, pop-style marketing, but this wasn't the first time Bezos had spoken with his customers directly. In fact, he does it quite often. Even a company as large as Amazon is willing to do offbeat things to communicate specific aspects of its character—that it is passionate about books and reading, for instance—to its customers.

You see, Bezos doesn't care how his message resonates with people looking for the cheapest product or wanting to save $2 on something they can buy elsewhere. He'll get those customers anyway; they're shoppers. Bezos is more interested in connecting with the customers who share similar *character* traits with Amazon—those who have the potential to become loyal to Amazon and the ability to increase profits over the long run. Amazon has created an authentic character, and the company takes great strides to perpetuate a few key points it wants to stick with its key customers. Are you trying to resonate with all of your customers, or the right ones?

Throughout my work coaching and mentoring more than 700 entrepreneurs and solo professionals, many of whom are building their personal brands to support the sale of their products or services, I quickly realized that character is just as important as the content they provide. I also realized early on that certain rules have to be followed—almost religiously—if an individual wanted to build and grow a strong personal brand. As my focus shifted from entrepreneurs and small businesses to larger companies, I saw the principle of character being used by some of the most successful large companies, such as Amazon, Apple, and Harley-Davidson. Furthermore, they are all Evergreen because of it!

THE POWER OF TELLING A GOOD STORY

Branding experts love to say that good branding is all about having a story. And it is true. Stories are, indeed, one of the most effective ways to make a business stick in the customer's mind. Look at any business that has been even remotely successful, and I'm willing to bet that you know quite a bit about its backstory. Let me give you an example.

These two guys got their start putting together computers in a garage, and they started one of the largest and most successful companies ever. Do you recognize them? I'm sure you do. You instantly know that I'm referring to Steve Jobs and Steve Wozniak, two of the three founders of Apple, because of a single line of backstory.

Chip and Dan Heath's must-read book, *Made to Stick: Why Some Ideas Survive and Others Die*, suggests that stories are one of the most important elements of any message that you want to stick. In business, this could not be more true. But the story itself is only part of the equation. Let's look at another example. What comes to mind if I mention a teenage kid who was bitten by a spider while on a school trip to a science lab and woke up the following day with the ability to climb buildings and swing from rooftop to rooftop? With a single line of backstory, you instantly know I'm referring to Spider-Man. How? Because this story involves a unique and well-developed character.

Fascinating characters are the crux of most compelling stories. They are the reason great works of fiction are so memorable. Authors take care to hone the backgrounds of their characters and ensure they are consistent with their actions in the story. Avid readers, in turn, discuss character development and are pleased when authors spend time developing their characters. Getting back to business, let's take a deeper look at our first example.

Apple has always positioned itself as a company that invites its customers to "think different"—a company that challenges the status quo. And even almost forty years ago, when the two Steves were in that garage, they understood that an "us vs. them" position was critical to both their story and their business success. Jobs also understood the principle of character. He made this statement in a 2004 *Businessweek* interview:

> When I got back here, Apple had forgotten who we were. Remember that "Think Different" ad campaign we ran [featuring great innovators from Einstein to Muhammad Ali to Gandhi]. It was certainly for customers to some degree, but it was even more for Apple itself....You

can tell a lot about a person by who his or her heroes are. That ad was to remind us of who our heroes are and who we are. We forgot that for a while.[2]

Character is the cornerstone of effective branding and one of the most critical components of an Evergreen business. Do you know who *you* are?

Remember, *you* are your own company's author. You are the one who can define its character and articulate other details to tell a vivid, engaging, and memorable story about your company. Don't leave this process up to the marketplace. Use historical and other tidbits to help make your character more refined, your story more compelling. When well crafted, this story will become part of the lore of your organization. Are *you* writing your company's story, or is it being written for you?

BUILDING THE CHARACTER
OF YOUR ORGANIZATION

Companies that are able to develop and live by the character they define connect with their customers on a deeper and more meaningful level than those that don't. Customers who are connected with an organization will feel a sense of purpose or belonging when they do business with it. This is where customer loyalty begins—long before the first sale is ever made. It is counterintuitive, because most companies think loyalty is something that happens after the sale. But what if you could do a lot of the heavy lifting before a customer even becomes a customer? Sounds good, right? So how, exactly, do you go about building the character of your organization?

In Simon Sinek's fantastic book, *Start with Why: How Great Leaders Inspire Everyone to Take Action*, he argues that most companies employ marketing practices—promotions, coupons, discounts, and the like— that, in essence, aim to manipulate the customer. Truly great companies, on the other hand, take a different tack: They aim to inspire the customer.

Inspired customers spread the word about a company and tell others. They are more prone to trust and believe what a company says and does, and they are more likely to remain loyal.

I can hear you now. "That sounds great, Noah, but I sell life insurance. Do you have any suggestions about how I can inspire my customers?" Sinek suggests that companies must start, as the title claims, by asking why. Why does your company do what it does? Sinek presents a concept that he calls the Golden Circle. He challenges you, the reader, to articulate your business model, starting at the core of the circle and defining *why* you do what you do, then (moving to the surrounding ring) defining *what* you do, and finally (moving to the outer ring) defining *how* you do it. As Sinek suggests, everything you do starts with asking why.

I agree with Sinek's premise, and would add that your content— shorthand used to describe what you do, sell, or provide—is really secondary to why it is that you do, sell, or provide that thing. To illustrate this concept, let's take a quick look at two companies that took differing approaches—and achieved wildly differing results.

Starting with "What"—a Failed Strategy

Many companies believe that *what* they make, sell, or provide is the most important component of their success. And sometimes they focus on this belief to the exclusion of everything else. Rewind a few years. What if you thought a new tablet would become an instant success if it was capable of supporting Flash (a technology Steve Jobs vehemently disagreed with, by the way)? What if it additionally had the ability to multitask on a handheld device? What if it also offered a gyroscope, a magnetometer, *and* an accelerometer? Would these features give the tablet a leg up on the already-established iPad? One company thought so....

In 2011, after more than $205 million had been invested in research and development, BlackBerry Ltd. was preparing for the launch of its first tablet, the PlayBook. But BlackBerry had a problem. Executives within the company disagreed about the product's target market. *Who* would actually want to buy this thing—*this product that had already been built?* This was a major operational blunder from a company that, for a short time, had dominated the mobile world with its e-mail platform.[3]

While BlackBerry executives were bickering about who would buy the PlayBook, they should have been spending the time to figure out who the company was—or, more precisely, *why* it was doing what it was doing.

Starting with "Why"—a Winning Strategy

Given the previous example, doesn't it make sense to truly understand **who** you are as an organization, *why* you do what you do, and ensure that you are able to effectively communicate these values at every opportunity and customer interaction with your company? It not only makes sense, but doing so will drastically change your business. Let me show you how.

When you, as a customer, buy a product or use a service from an organization that understands the principle of character, you almost subconsciously step into a role very closely associated with the character of the company from which we are buying. So when you buy an iPhone, for example, you're not just buying an iPhone. You're stepping into an association with the "us vs. them" character that Apple has carefully created and nurtured over the years.

Finding the Sweet Spot

When a company is able to match how it sees itself with how it sees the customer, and with how the customer sees the company, an awesome synergy occurs. This is the power of character—where customer loyalty starts. This is the sweet spot. Companies that recognize this sweet spot—and that spend their time, money, and resources focused here—waste very little money on how they communicate with or market to prospective and existing customers. They waste far less money on customer acquisition adventures. And when a company defines its character, it has a simple, one-question diagnostic tool it can use to measure any outward communication with prospective or existing customers: Does this [fill in the blank: advertisement, e-mail, tweet, letter, etc.] match how we want to be seen and perceived by our customers?

Do you see why Apple is a great example? Apple has never been in the product business. It's been in the business of selling the character of Apple. Buying your first Apple product is a bit like eating the forbidden fruit. Once you've had a bite, you're hooked. And this happens because Apple is so clear about who it is and how it wants customers to see the company. This allows Apple to tailor messages specifically toward the customers it is trying to reach. Marketing is no longer guesswork.

BlackBerry might introduce a device that's able to multitask better than the iPad. Microsoft might introduce what it coins as a "game-changing tablet" loaded with new features or a third camera. Google might introduce a gizmo loaded with features that blows away anything Apple has ever created. We might even buy those products, but they won't win our loyalty too easily. Customer loyalty isn't won or created through content (the thing your company does, sells, or provides). Loyalty is created through careful application of the principle of character and the principle of community. Your content merely supports the root structure of a towering Evergreen.

DISTINGUISHING BETWEEN
CHARACTER AND CARICATURE

Have you set up your Facebook profile? I'm not talking about your business for a moment, I'm asking about *you* personally. Are you one of the 1.28 billion users who is using Facebook?[4] The problem with Facebook is that it has become somewhat of a vanity-publishing platform for hundreds of millions of people—a soapbox, if you will. Each day I watch hundreds of acquaintances—some I haven't seen in ten, fifteen, twenty, or more years—share everything about their lives. They share pictures,

...hen they are home (and when they're not, to the praise ...rglars everywhere),[5] what they ate for dinner, when their dog had bladder stones removed, and when little Billy threw his peas on the floor. My wife refers to Facebook as Bragbook. She remains one of the small number of people left on the planet who refuses to set up a Facebook account. She has a point, because while many people are living their lives and using Facebook as a tool to stay connected, many others are living a secondary, more virtual, Facebook life. Facebook allows people to fictitiously engineer the way in which they present themselves to the world and how they are perceived.

Perhaps I'm being overly cynical and harsh. After all, Facebook has become one of the primary ways in which people stay connected. It also allows companies to engage with existing customers and reach new customers through platforms like Facebook for Business. Most companies, though, like most people, tend to put their best "face" on Facebook. My friend Samar Bechara, a technology consultant from Lebanon, says, "Facebook is for socializing like pornography is for love. A fake, cheap substitute for the real deal." It's a fantastic analogy, and it's hard to argue with him. Instead of settling for using Facebook as a tool to seduce your customers, use it as a tool to engage your customers.

Here's my advice for an organization that wants to use the legitimate communication advantages that Facebook for Business has to offer: Stop spending so much time presenting what I call the "Facebook You" and start seriously developing the "Real You." So many marketing teams fail to grasp this one important point. If a company spends time and money trying to sell customers on a glorified representation of who it actually is and what it stands for, those marketing efforts are almost all guaranteed to fail. That's not character; it's caricature.

In Japan, there are two popular terms used to describe this phenomenon. The Japanese refer to it as *omote-ura*. *Omote* (the public face) refers to the way a company or person wishes to be seen by the outside world. It's seen as a mixture of reality, myth, and lies. *Ura* (the private face) is the reality behind the *omote*.[6] Is your company presenting its true character, or a caricature of how you want to be perceived by the outside world? Beware: If you are presenting a caricature of how you think the market wants to see you (your *omote*), you'll never build authentic customer loyalty.

The same marketers who tend to fall into this trap frequently tout concepts such as "transparency," a common buzzword in the marketing world. The problem with transparency, however, is that companies and experts alike haven't truly defined what it means—and how it can help grow a business. I'm not in a position to attempt to resolve this issue here. I can tell you, however, with a great degree of certainty, a few things that transparency is *not*. It's not about sharing every detail about your company, regardless of security and confidentiality issues. It's not about designating a group of employees or hiring a social media team whose sole mission is to respond or engage the moment someone gives your brand a nudge or mention on the Web. It's not about being reactive.

Let's consider an alternative—being *proactive*, which all Evergreen companies are. The "Facebook You" representation of your brand doesn't work because it isn't authentic to who you really are, and *why* you really do what you do. As such, this approach will only get you so far. Customers see right through companies that only take part to push offers in an effort to stimulate sales. Sure, you may generate some "likes," and you may encourage some limited engagement, but this is not an effective strategy for building a following of loyal customers. Rather than creating a caricature of yourself, don't you think it makes more sense to figure out who you actually are, thereby allowing your prospects and customers to connect in a more meaningful and impactful way?

ARTICULATING THE "REAL YOU"

Let's now focus on a simple process for learning more about who your company really is, what exactly you stand for, and the type of brand personality you want customers to associate with your organization. From there, I'll show you how to marry those key character attributes to what it is you actually do. I've helped numerous companies make tremendous strides in their marketing and loyalty efforts by simply helping them clarify their authentic character—and once they do, sparks fly, results increase, and their success is dramatic. But before we turn to how your company can apply these practices, let's take a quick look at two successful examples that have already demonstrated how this idea works.

Learning from Zappos

Zappos, an online retailer that specializes in shoes, has taken great care to embed its character within every aspect of the shopping experience. Whether or not they purchase items, visitors can't help but walk away from their interaction with the site having a strong impression of the company. Here's one way Zappos does it: Nearly every pair of shoes available on the website is accompanied by a video created by a different Zappos employee who describes the shoes in great detail, from the tread on the bottom to those little plastic tips on the ends of the shoelaces. These videos successfully communicate two things about Zappos employees: They are as passionate about shoes as they are about the customers' shopping experience.

At the same time, these videos present the company's key character traits, the main one being that Zappos is the most customer service–friendly company on the planet. It's also the happiest place to work, because pleasing the customer is the number one goal. These key points are communicated through each and every interaction and message. Get the idea? Now, how could *you* ensure that you are always enunciating your character traits in everyday interactions with your company?

Learning from Jamie Oliver

When sous chef Jamie Oliver was discovered and given his own cooking show by the BBC in 1997, he became known as "The Naked Chef." This was certainly a clever, attention-grabbing name for a decent-looking, late-twentysomething chef with a unique approach to preparing simple, fun, and healthy meals—and he quickly attracted millions of fans in the United Kingdom. Oliver's rise to celebrity chef stardom eventually brought him to the United States, where he found even greater opportunity. Oliver has executed crusades against everything from the fast-food industry to the poor nutritional quality of food served in school cafeterias.

Controversy sells. Oliver has become one of the most influential food personalities in the world.[7] He has also become the second-richest author in Britain.[8] Likewise, Oliver's personal brand has exploded. Today he's a household name, with his branding on everything from pasta sauce to noodles and pots and pans. Let's take a behind-the-scenes look at how Oliver's marketing team orchestrates this phenomenal success.

In *Jamie Oliver: Fresh Retail Ventures Brand Guidelines*, a page with the heading "Our Values and Personality" details precise rules that must be followed for communicating on behalf of the Oliver brand. It reads: "Jamie is known for his warm personality, strong beliefs, and enthusiasm for sharing knowledge."[9] It goes on to characterize his personality as "honest and challenging—being direct, open-minded, and genuine; passionate and inspiring—true excitement and love for food and healthy living; approachable and fun—unpretentious, accessible, and playful, encouraging everyone to have a go." A few pages later, under the heading "Tone of Voice," it's explained that words must be "filled with Jamie's easy warmth" and that "copy should always be a balance between purpose and passion, sharing knowledge and opinions in a truly engaging way that resonates with all people." This is exactly the sort of clarity you need in creating your own corporate character.

Bringing These Strategies Back to You

It doesn't matter that you're not one of the most influential food personalities or the second-highest-paid author in Britain. The same type of clarity that Oliver's marketing team articulated in their branding efforts is required for your business—regardless of its size, what industry you're in, or how many employees you have. This clarity is accessible to any kind of business and will have dramatic impact on the effectiveness of your marketing efforts and your ability to build relationships with your customers.

The process of clearly articulating the character of a business makes communicating easier for everyone within the organization. It also helps mitigate the chance that people will muck things up. This is precisely why companies create brand guidelines. So now let me ask you a question: If you're a small business, let's say with twenty or so employees, what distinguishes your business from your competitors? Don't you think clarity about your character would make everything—from in-store customer service to the way the phones are answered—work just a little bit better? Of course it would! And these are the things that help you retain customers and create greater customer loyalty. There's no sense fixing how customers are greeted or how the phones are answered if it's incongruent with the character traits you've presented and the expectations you've built about your brand. Let's work on creating *your* character now.

CREATING YOUR CORPORATE CHARACTER

Does your company have a mission statement or a value proposition that encompasses the core of what you do? In skyscrapers everywhere, gorgeous bronze plaques adorn the walls of companies with words that are supposed to describe the essence of who those companies are, how they do what they do, and why they do it. The problem is that most missions, values, and visions don't match the day-to-day actions of the employees of the company. The reason is that most mission statements and value propositions are created based on what the company thinks the customer wants or expects to hear, and most actions that are intended to carry out those words are done so haphazardly.

By contrast, when your corporate character is in alignment with the words in the mission statement on your office wall, and when the day-to-day actions of your staff are similarly in alignment with your character, you create an organization-wide cornerstone for providing greater customer service and connecting with customers on a deeper and more meaningful level. Your goal must be to move away from generating transactions and toward creating connections. You want customers to accept who you are. And in so doing, you want to be able to influence them and their decisions.

Every brand has personality, but most companies aren't sure what that personality is and how to consistently communicate it with customers at every point of interaction. On the pages that follow, you'll find a starter guide to creating your company's persona. Most branding experts will guide you through a process of answering questions such as, "If you were a car, what would you be?" Or, "What kind of movie is your company?" That line of questioning can be somewhat helpful, but I believe there's a more effective way; it's the same way I help my own clients.

There is a five-step process that I use to build a company's character. These steps also, in my opinion, articulate the most important components of a strong corporate character.

At this point I'd like you to roll up your sleeves and try a few short brainstorming exercises. You can do these exercises with your team, as a group, or by yourself. As you make your way through these exercises you'll start to see how this process builds a rich, fascinating character unlike any you've likely considered. As you follow the five-step process, you can write down your answer to each question or simply ponder the question.

Step One: Develop Your Origin Story

In this day and age, your customers are continuously bombarded by information and messages. It is all too easy for them to forget what your company does, and how it does it. Remember, stories resonate and stick—so tell them! If your company started in a garage, then say so. Build a rich and complex backstory about your company and communi-

&

customers. No detail is too small. Your customers want to

his story will help create a connection.

y answering the following questions:

- Who started the company?

- When was it started? Where? How?

- Why was it started?

- What were the original visions or aspirations for the company?

- What traditions has the company maintained since it began?

Take a moment now and write a paragraph or two about your company. Don't overthink it. Just write about your company using the answers you gave to the previous questions.

Step Two: Define Your Superhero

People want to do business with people and companies they like and trust, but more important, they want to do business with people who fascinate them. Superheroes fascinate us. It's the reason we remember the backstories of the human beings who became Spider-Man, Batman, and Iron Man. Imagine your company as a superhero. By building your company's core message and vision around the personality of a larger-than-life character, you'll resonate on a much more meaningful level with your ideal customer.

Not all characters have to be superheroes in the literal sense. Many companies have been successfully built on the persona or personality of real-life "heroes." Consider characters such as Colonel Sanders of Kentucky Fried Chicken, Orville Redenbacher, or Richard Branson from Virgin Group. I'm not saying you need to rush out and create a mascot or put your owner's face on everything. Far from it. The main thing to remember is this: The personality of your character must be perpetuated through every employee, every piece of marketing, and every bit of customer communication.

Above all else, however, your company's character needs to be *fascinating*. Boring people don't command our attention or respect. Companies are no different. We are attracted to certain people because they excite and fascinate us. We're attracted to certain companies because they make us wonder, *What are they going to do next?* The character of Apple fascinates people. So does that of Southwest Airlines, Harley-Davidson, and Disney. When was the last time you saw people lined up at the Microsoft store, or heard a friend confess that she was up late scouring the Internet for leaked photos of the latest Windows Phone? My point exactly.

In step one of this exercise, you created a paragraph describing the origin story of your company. Now I want you to create a superhero and write a narrative about your company that excites and fascinates both customers and those working within your organization. Typically, most companies describe themselves in a pretty bland manner. Your origin story needs to include a character that's larger than life. This is the mythology of your legend. Bruce Wayne dedicated his life to avenging crime because he witnessed the murder of his parents as they exited the theater on that fateful night. So what's your reason for providing amazing health care, or tire rotations, or gourmet hot dogs, or accounting services? What makes *you* unique?

Try this. Ask yourself the following questions about your company:

- What is your superpower?

- What does your organization do better than anyone else?

- What challenges did your organization overcome to get where it is today?

- What failures did you experience along the way?

- What adventures did you have?

- What are your likes, dislikes, or pet peeves?

Now try writing a simple paragraph about your company that's actually exciting. And don't draft the typical "About Us" copy. Have a little fun. If you want to see a fantastic real-life example, take a look at the website for the accounting firm of Macias Gini & O'Connell LLP (MGO).[10] Accounting—and, by extension, accountants—are boring, right? If you concur with this traditional typecast, think again. These guys are anything but boring, and they've taken great strides to make sure you know it. They've built a really fascinating character for the typical accountant. Take a look at all the benefits of being boring—and then ponder how *you* can jazz up your image.

Step Three: Build Purpose for Your Character's Actions

The next step in crafting your character is understanding your company's purpose for doing what it does. Define your raison d'être. Anytime you communicate with your customers, you must have strategic intent. If you don't have a valid reason to communicate with a customer, don't do it. If your message has excess verbiage that doesn't serve a purpose, lose it.

Whatever you do, or whatever you say, it must be consistent with who you are and how you want to be known—but most important, it must have a purpose. In Chapter 1, I said that most companies spend time trying to game and manipulate things (like figuring out the best time to send an e-mail) without first deciding if they have something purposeful to say. Every time you communicate with your customers make sure to put your messaging through a "smell test." Smell it! Does the message match up with who you are, and how you want your customers to perceive you—or does it stink like thinly veiled manipulative marketing? Giving purpose to your character is about adding context.

Spend a few minutes answering the following questions about your company:

- Who are you and what do you want to be known for?

- What are the key points you want customers to associate with you?

- What's your larger-than-life purpose? For example, is it to build products that change the world?

- Who are your enemies? (They might be competitors or bigger issues, such as poor design.)

- What rules do you live by?

- What kind of legacy do you want to leave?

Challenge yourself to truly consider your reasons for doing what you do. Now write a paragraph that summarizes that raison d'être.

Step Four: Create an Avatar of Your Character

Now that you've built a fascinating backstory and persona, and articulated your purpose, it's time to create an actual avatar of what your character looks like. Specifically, I want you to describe the person who has lived, or is living, this fascinating story. Here are a few questions to get you started:

- Is your avatar male or female?

- How old is he or she?

- Where was he or she born?

- What type of education does he or she have?

- How would you describe your avatar's personality?

- What words would you use to describe his or her tone of voice?

- What does your avatar do on the weekend or when there's free time?

- How would your avatar's friends or family members describe him or her?

I'm sure you get the idea. You can continue to ask questions about your character's personality type until you have a clear vision of this avatar in your head. Then try writing a description of your avatar in 100 words or less.

Step Five: Translate Your Vision to the Voice of Your Customer

Imagine that your company's character and your ideal customer met today for the first time. Could you write a conversation that might transpire between them? Peter Drucker wrote, "The aim of marketing is to know and understand the customer so well that the product/service fits him and sells itself."[11] This exercise is about gaining that level of knowledge and understanding.

Ask yourself the following questions:

- How would they introduce themselves?

- How would they describe themselves to each other?

- What would they talk about?

- What would the conversation be like?

This exercise might seem like an easy one to skip over, but I've seen some incredible results when people have spent time on this step. So why not give it a shot? Try this: Craft a fictional conversation between your corporate character and your ideal customer. If they don't have anything to say to one another and there are moments of awkward silence, then I'm afraid you have more work to do. But don't worry. In Chapter 6, we will discuss at length why you need to articulate your ideal customer's character (and how, strategically, you should go about this process), so for now, just take a stab at capturing the two voices and the gist of their dialogue.

CHAPTER 4

Examining the Principle
of Community

Creating a Forest from a Single Seed

In 2000, Greg Glassman set out to change organized fitness—specifically the way humans increase their strength, endurance, physical capacity, and athletic performance. He developed workouts that contain a variety of unique exercise movements, including everything from doing push-ups, lifting weights, and rowing to flipping tires, shoveling snow, and pulling sleds. CrossFit has become a monster-size brand—one that has turned the world of organized fitness and training upside down. Today, there are more than 8,500 CrossFit gyms around the globe. CrossFit has built a community with hundreds of thousands (and perhaps even millions) of members covering virtually every square inch of the planet.[1]

How could a company experience such dramatic growth so quickly? The answer, quite simply, is that CrossFit embraced the principle of community from an early stage and has constantly improved, evolved, and increased how its community interacts—both online and off-line. What started with a single website and a small component of what we could consider a virtual community, CrossFit has evolved to include meet-ups, gatherings, and competitions where CrossFit names the "Fittest Man (and Woman) on Earth." The CrossFit brand encompasses a for-profit journal with high-quality content, a thriving discussion board, and, of course, more than 8,500 independently owned and operated gyms around the world.

CrossFit literally took on a life of its own—one that not even Glassman could have slowed down if he had wanted to. In this case, the community grew the brand; the brand didn't grow the community. Most companies aren't fortunate enough to have their communities grow their brands to this magnitude, but even a small business can create a vibrant community.

WHY SHOULD *YOU* BUILD A COMMUNITY?

Organizations that successfully build customer communities experience remarkable benefits from their efforts. More to the point, however, I believe companies no longer have a choice—particularly not if we want to excel and experience exponential growth. As our customers are becoming more interconnected, they are naturally beginning to build elements of community on their own. Furthermore, if you don't create a strong customer community, you can be guaranteed that your competitors will.

Creating a winning customer community takes time and money. There's no doubt about it. But remember what I told you in Chapter 1? So much money is wasted on customer acquisition escapades when it could be better invested elsewhere. It only makes sense to spend that money (at least a good portion of it) on deepening your relationships with existing customers. This is what community is all about—building and strengthening those relationships.

I have to tell you right upfront: Pulling it off will take a massive companywide commitment. And you can't give up when the going gets tough. But if you do it right, your community will become the linchpin of unbreakable customer loyalty and an unmistakable competitive advantage.

In my work with clients, I've come to recognize five distinct benefits that come from building customer communities. They are:

1. *Dramatically Improved Customer Value.* Quite simply, with increased customer loyalty, increased perception of your brand, and improved connection with your customers comes greater revenues and healthier profits.

2. *More Effective Referral Generation.* Many organizations attempt to foster word-of-mouth through their marketing programs. My experience has shown that organizations with strong customer communities experience more authentic and organic word-of-mouth. In a nutshell, your customers begin to do the work you used to do.

3. *Greater Understanding of Your Customers' Voice.* If your community is thriving and your structures allow for open and ongoing dialogue, you'll have a true understanding of your customers' experiences, thoughts, and feelings about your company. This type of insight allows executives and management to make effective decisions, at every level of the organization, in line with customer feedback.

4. *Improved Customer Service and Support.* Here's an interesting phenomenon: As connection to the brand and community increases, customer support and service requests may actually decrease. Customers often take on the role of problem solver or service provider. Furthermore, they are more likely to brush aside a bad experience as an anomaly, more willing to forgive and forget, and far less likely to spread negativity.

5. *Increased Customer-Focused Culture.* As you begin to build your customer community, you'll find your employees will become clearer about and have greater understanding of your business's character, which in turn creates an increasingly customer-focused culture. Those within the organization will work together to solve customer issues and create a greater and more enriched customer experience. Entire departments will begin to work together. A fierce customer community ensures that everyone within the organization knows what customers are saying and why. More important, your customers understand that they've been heard and that their opinions are valued.

As you can see, some pretty powerful outcomes can result from building a customer community. I hope that I've convinced you to stop asking, "Should we build a customer community?" and instead gotten you to start asking, "When, where, and how do we start?" If so, read on! But before you begin creating your community, you need to know what a community is—and, more important, what it is not.

THE DIFFERENCE BETWEEN
A TRIBE AND A COMMUNITY

Marketers love to talk about "tribes." Prolific author and thought leader Seth Godin first used the term as a business analogy in his book of the same name (*Tribes: We Need You to Lead Us*). There he argues that success in an increasingly connected world comes from finding and cultivating your tribe—your legion of followers. Godin suggests that the future of companies and individuals will be determined by how well they build and connect with their tribes. I respect Godin tremendously and have learned much from him over the past decade. While having dinner together a few years ago, he quizzed me about my own tribe. Since that night, though, I've wondered whether he really meant "communities" when he said "tribes."

Alan Weiss—probably the most prolific consultant on the planet, author of more than fifty books (as well as the foreword to this one), and a thought leader of the same caliber as Godin—confirmed what I was thinking. He suggested to me that Godin may have painted himself into a corner by using the wrong term. Weiss believes that tribes are homogenous, whereas communities are heterogeneous. He wrote a very interesting post that elaborates on his view:

> Tribes are exclusionary. They recognize their own members' similarities and common background, and tend to take captives or slaves, generally seeing others as enemies at worst and inferiors at best. A famous experiment with devoted Starbucks users and Dunkin' Donuts users found that no one in either group would agree to switch brands or environment—they were true tribes, derogatory and condescending about the other. ("I felt I was intruding in someone's fancy living room in Starbucks." "Do you realize that in Dunkin' Donuts you can't get soy milk in your latté?")
>
> Communities are inclusionary. They are characterized by common attitudes, interests, and goals. Religion, beliefs, kinship, and opinions can differ starkly in communities and, in fact, give them vibrancy and dynamism, allowing for continued experimentation and growth. They do not hold long-term animosities against other communities, and those within them shift in opinion and allegiance as time goes by and learning occurs.[2]

Godin and Weiss both make interesting points, and I actually think they are both right. You can build a tribe, or you can build a community. However, you need to be deliberate in your actions because they are not the same, and each requires very different tactical and strategic considerations. This is not generally understood. In fact, most otherwise-savvy marketers who talk about their tribe-building efforts are actually building communities or vice versa. Confused? Don't be. You'll start to understand as we examine one well-known and popular tribe.

Learning from Abercrombie & Fitch—a Quintessential Tribe

If you've ever walked into an Abercrombie & Fitch store, you know immediately whether you fit into its tribe. Real people stand in the windows, acting as live mannequins; every employee somehow looks the same (guys are buff, with chiseled chins, and the girls seem to have come straight out of *Seventeen* magazine); music pulsates through the store. Like McDonald's, an Abercrombie in Detroit looks no different from an Abercrombie in San Francisco. These affectations are deliberate attempts to make certain people feel comfortable and energized, and others excluded.

Abercrombie goes to great lengths to build its tribe in this manner. And it works. Every time I've entered one of these stores it is packed with teenage boys and girls who are piling the debt on Mom and Dad's credit cards. Most of the kids shopping at Abercrombie resemble the employees who are helping them find the right size pants.

For me, walking into an Abercrombie is not a comfortable fit. Will they take my money, as an outsider? Sure. A&F is more than happy to have a transactional relationship with someone like me. But I'll never associate and connect with the tribe like someone who matches the corporate character that Abercrombie is working to have a relationship with.

Marketers who want to build a tribe use aspects of the principle of character. They know it's not as important for their company to resonate with everyone as it is to ensure that it resonates with the customers with whom they are trying to connect. They are very clear about who fits well into their group, who they are marketing to, and who has the greatest potential of becoming loyal to their brand. These marketers take great care in tailoring their customer experience toward the ideal customer. There's no mistaking it; Abercrombie is entirely sure about its intent. This is tribal mentality at its best, and it's hard to argue with the success of Abercrombie & Fitch.

The Tribe Leader's Mistake

Rewind a few years. Abercrombie & Fitch, a company with a long history, found itself on the brink of bankruptcy close to the date of its 100th birthday. Limited Brands purchased the company and decided to make apparel the main focus. The new management hired the young, energetic Mike Jeffries and put him in charge of reinvigorating the brand.[3] Jeffries knew exactly the type of company he wanted to build: He became obsessed with generating a "sexy and emotional experience" for customers. According to one article, "When he took the reins of the company with the moose logo in 1992, thirty-six stores generated approximately $50 million in annual sales. By 2012 the company had grown to include more than 1,000 stores with annual sales surpassing $4.5 billion."[4]

The rise was astonishing. Jeffries, however, took his obsession a bit too far. He made headlines in early 2013 when some shocking things that he had said a few years earlier made their way into the media. In 2006, Jeffries had commented that Abercrombie specifically marketed only to "cool and good-looking people."[5] While remarks like this seem odd, harming, and disgraceful—which by any stretch of the imagination they are—he was actually simply saying that Abercrombie is exclusionary. This, by definition, is the very nature of a tribe.

On the surface, Jeffries's comments may have simply been honest; he was articulating the customers he wanted to attract and develop a long-term relationship with. His critical error, though, was that you can't be super obvious about your intent when you're solely focused on building a tribe, unless you are able to do it altruistically. Being exclusionary is okay, and in some cases the more exclusionary the better, but to outright say that "we don't want a huge segment of the population to shop here because they might not be their ideal weight, super popular, or the best-looking kid in the class"—this kind of comment does more damage than good to the well-being of the brand.

Prior to Jeffries's comments, Abercrombie's success was impressive. Early 2014 revenues, however, show a decrease in sales.[6] The company announced it might have to cut pricing to try and win back teenage customers in an intensely competitive environment. Has the tribe leader's mistake caught up with him? Time will tell. Thankfully, there's a better way.

THE CROSSFIT COMMUNITY

So let's get back to Greg Glassman's story. When he founded CrossFit Inc. and CrossFit.com, he did so because he believed strongly that traditional organized fitness was broken—and he was determined to change things. Glassman's response to the problem was the CrossFit model, which he developed based on "constantly varied, high-intensity, functional movements."[7] My jujitsu instructor first introduced me to CrossFit in 2006. After my first workout, which consisted of a half dozen rounds of 200-meter sprints and 21 kettlebell swings, I vomited all over the road.

My puking episode is considered to be an initiation ritual into the world of CrossFit. In fact, CrossFit's own mascot is named Pukie. Pukie is a cartoon clown who, having just completed a CrossFit workout, is crouching over and vomiting violently. Another caricature, described as Uncle Rhabdo, shows a clown who has contracted rhabdomyolysis, or "rhabdo." (Rhabdomyolysis—which occurs when muscles are worked so hard that the fibers break down, releasing the protein myoglobin into the bloodstream—is a health concern that's become associated with CrossFit over the years. In extreme cases, it can lead to kidney failure.) Badly bruised and totally exhausted, Uncle Rhabdo is shown hooked up to a dialysis machine with his kidneys and intestines hanging out.

On the surface, you might not consider these to be the best character portrayals of an organization, but here's the interesting thing: Loyal fans and "customers" of CrossFit recognize these characters as satirical caricatures designed to remind them to slow down and not kill themselves while following a CrossFit training regimen. In short, CrossFit's community has embraced these two clowns.

How CrossFit Built Its Community

The CrossFit model is simple. Every day, people from all over the world visit CrossFit.com, where Glassman and his team post a Workout of the Day, or WOD. Anyone can look each day (at Crossfit.com, for free), complete the workout, and share results. You don't need to be a paying member to take part in the community. Many CrossFit junkies still complete their daily workouts in their home garages and enjoy all the benefits that come along with participating in the community. Others prefer to pay to visit one of CrossFit's independently owned CrossFit gyms. As Cross-Fit's community grew, so did the size of the brand—exponentially.

In the early days of CrossFit, the daily workout was posted on the website (referred to as the "main site"—you'll see why this is important in a moment). Individuals completed workouts on their own and then reported back to CrossFit.com, sharing their times or scores on the individual tasks. As months passed, members started to benchmark themselves against each other. Then they discussed movements, form, and technique. And then—while members remained competitive and mostly self-interested in the massive personal gains they derived from taking part—they started cultivating a natural instinct to push each other, to hold each other accountable, and to strive for the greater good of others. The community was born.

As the CrossFit brand grew, the model morphed, but it continued to rely more on the people and less on the equipment. For example, organized CrossFit gyms routinely meet in a local park, parking lot, or track. It doesn't matter. Can you imagine paying a monthly gym fee and going to an empty warehouse with nothing more than a couple of pull-up bars, some weights, and a lot of open space? This is part of CrossFit's brilliance. There are no mirrors, no vast lines of elliptical machines with built-in channel changers, no televisions, no "healthy smoothies" to be consumed after your workout.

When members go to CrossFit, they are there to do two things: Complete a WOD and take part in the community. They're not there to increase just their own strength, but also the collective strength of the community. CrossFit members pay hefty fees to their gym, but they also take pride in their ownership of that space. They clean up after a workout and keep the place tidy and clean. And when a member is the last person to complete the WOD, he or she doesn't need to fret. Soon a dozen people will be cheering their fellow CrossFit member on. I've seen it happen, numerous times.

Glassman started CrossFit in 2000 with a bare-bones website and a single gym in Santa Cruz, California, with very limited equipment. (The website hasn't drastically changed, by the way, nor has the process; you visit the website, you do the workout, you post your time.) In 2006 there were eighteen CrossFit gyms in the United States. As of this writing, there are more than 8,500 gyms worldwide. That's a 47,122 percent increase in just eight short years. This community started from a single seed and grew into an incredibly lush forest.

Cultivating Tribe Lingo

During its community-building endeavors, CrossFit embraced certain aspects of a tribe mentality. For instance, tribes often use very specific language, which simultaneously generates a sense of connection and exclusion. Only members "in the club" truly understand what the language means and how to use it. CrossFit has done this exceptionally well. Examples of CrossFit's language include:

- *WOD:* Workout of the Day. "Have you completed the WOD yet?" "Today's WOD is ..."

- *AMRAP:* As Many Rounds/Reps As Possible. "Complete AMRAP of 5 pull-ups, 10 push-ups, and 16 squats in 20 minutes."

- *Fran, Angie, Barbie, Cindy, Grace, and others:* The Benchmark Girls. These workouts, with female names, are some of the hardest CrossFit has to offer. Cindy, for example, requires you to complete 5 pull-ups, 10 push-ups, and 15 squats with AMRAP in 20 minutes.

- *Box:* A CrossFit facility. "My box has about thirty members. You should come check it out."

- *Main Site:* Crossfit.com. Many of the 8,500 affiliate gyms also post a daily workout. When one CrossFitter asks another if he or she has completed the daily workout, the other person typically asks whether the fellow CrossFitter is following "main site WODs" or another source.

It's important to keep in mind that the language shared by a community often isn't created by the company, but rather by customers interacting with the brand. That said, if your customers create the language, it's up to you to be aware of what's happening and to begin using the language as a part of your daily lexicon. Do *your* customers use specific language and lingo during their interactions with your organization? If not, could you build words, short forms, or phrases around your products and services?

Embracing Tribal Tactics

Similar to Apple, CrossFit maintains a stringent "us vs. them" mentality that creates a more tribal than communal atmosphere. CrossFit has maintained a long-standing battle with the standard organized fitness industry. Its members refer to normal, everyday gyms as "globo gyms"—the typical big-box gym where guys spend more time looking in the mirror doing bicep curls than they do actually getting into shape. Brand communities derive power from being exclusionary. It's important to be insular. But real power comes from also remaining open and welcoming to newcomers.

Those who are even mildly enchanted by the idea of CrossFit are usually hooked after the first WOD. There's something special about a workout that takes your body to the brink of exhaustion. I was both an avid and a rabid member of the CrossFit community for years. My wife maintains that it seems to be more exclusionary, cult-oriented, and tribal than community-focused, but I disagree. CrossFit's strength as an organization lies in the fact that it employs community structure using tribal tactics. The pain created by doing a four-minute Fran WOD, or pushing a tractor tire down the road, creates fierce camaraderie among CrossFit members. In return, they refer everyone they know and are relentless in trying to get them to join the community.

Okay, I guess that does sound like a cult, but CrossFit has done what most businesses wish they could do. CrossFit has created a devout community that in turn has translated into greater customer retention, incredible word-of-mouth, rapid growth, and extreme profits. It's hard to argue that this isn't a worthwhile goal for any organization. The question, though, is whether there is a systematic formula that an organization can follow to build a similar brand community.

The answer is yes, and I'll show you how it's done.

BUILDING YOUR CUSTOMER COMMUNITY

The success of customer communities comes from strong leadership, a forward-thinking vision, and the execution of a strategic plan. I'm going to help you develop your own roadmap.

Step One: Define Your Strategy

If you were to imagine a future where your organization had a thriving customer community, what would that look like? Here are a few questions to ask when developing your community strategy:

- What are your long-term objectives for your business? How do you envision a customer community helping you reach those objectives?

- What are your objectives for building a customer community?

- What would reaching those objectives mean to your organization? How would your organization benefit from a customer community?

- Who are the key decision makers within your organization that need to be on board with your community-building strategy?

- Is everyone within the organization committed to your customer community objectives and your desired future state? If not, how are you going to convince them it's time to get on board? (*Besides giving them this book!*)

- What issues or barriers might prevent you from building a customer community? How can you address those challenges?

- Whose budget will support building a customer community?

- Who will initially manage your community-building efforts?

The strategy for building a thriving customer community must start at the top and trickle down into every facet of your organization. This is why it is important to identify the decision makers who will drive this process—be they department managers, key executives, or others in the company. It's also why you must define your character first. Your corporate strategy is important, but your positioning, key character traits, mission, and values will drive your community efforts much further. Once you have defined your vision, you will more easily be able to define what community structures you need in place, and why, and how to effectively manage them.

One of the most famous examples of a successful brand community is Harley-Davidson. When Harley-Davidson found itself struggling in the early 1980s, a group of executives made a bid to purchase the company. Those executives decided to embrace the communities that already existed. They recognized how motorcycle club members and enthusiasts were attached to their motorcycles. They realized that a culture of loyalty already existed for the product, but not necessarily to their brand. Harley-Davidson sought to build itself as the company that not just made motorcycles, but that also truly understood the motorcyclists and the culture of riding.

This strategy and vision had legs—or perhaps wheels. But much like the CrossFit community, the Harley-Davidson community evolved on its own. Employees were required to run customer events, and this experience gave them a greater understanding of the customer's needs, desires, and aspirations. A direct line of customer feedback was born. Harley-Davidson embraced the relationship, showing customers what it really meant to be loved, and customers responded. Harley-Davidson is the largest motorcycle company in the world, with annual revenues in the billions of dollars. More important, by truly coming to grips with its own character, and with an accurate understanding of its most valuable customer, the company was able to put the structures in place to build one of the most emulated customer communities of our time.

Step Two: Choose Your Tools

Much like chasing the Holy Grail, many companies chase the Next Big Thing when it comes to building their communities. In today's day and age, social media is the Next Big Thing. Many experts out there promise organizations that social media will be the savior to all their customer communication goals. I have serious issues with sweeping assurances like that. Social media is important, yes—but it's not the most important consideration when crafting your community. Building a customer community doesn't mean you simply hop on the Web, create social media profiles on all the big sites (such as Facebook, Twitter, and Pinterest), or add a discussion forum or blog to your website and call it day. Yet these are the types of knee-jerk reactions made by leaders of organizations or folks in the marketing department when they decide that their companies would benefit from building a customer community. Many brands actually end up hurting themselves by jumping on the social wagon and using the tools to incessantly blast customers with new products and promotions.

Many social media experts claim that social media closes the feedback loop by providing us a way to be in touch with our customers and their needs, desires, and aspirations on a 24/7 basis. The problem, though, is that this logic confuses community building with customer feedback. Both are important, but they are entirely different animals. Obviously, a more effective feedback loop allows for a greater customer experience, and better customer service, but this is a poor substitute for building a customer community.

Online community building should, most likely, be only one small component of your overall community-building efforts. (Remember: The CrossFit community was primarily built off-line, and Harley-Davidson's community was built long before we had Twitter, Facebook, and Pinterest.) The most important question to ask yourself is: "Does this product/service/tool help us reach our overall community objectives?" If the answer is yes, by all means do it. But also ask yourself what else you can do to broaden the reach of these efforts.

The key here is simple: Don't be fooled that social media, or even the Internet for that matter, will be your shining light toward building a strong customer community. Understand the business you're in and the type of structures that would allow your brand to create a greater sense of community among your customers. It might all happen off-line. Don't be tricked into ignoring the humble local newspaper. Don't be tricked into ignoring the power of direct mail or a printed newsletter, either. The Web offers us tools, to be sure, but it is not the be-all and end-all solution.

Step Three: Cultivate Your Community (Not Just Your Brand)

In Chapter 3, I introduced the principle of character and said that it was similar to the concept of positioning, which brand experts have been talking about since before I was even born. The concept of positioning is simple: Companies need to find a way to differentiate their brand from those of their competition and continuously present that differentiation to customers in a way that connects and resonates with them.

Typically, communities are cultivated by bringing people together around shared interests, values, and beliefs, and that's fine. Take an online discussion forum, for example; there are millions and millions of them. You can find a group of people connected around any specific hobby, value, or belief that you could possibly imagine. Traditional brand "communities" are built under the assumption that it's enough for customers to simply be connected to a brand—that this connection, in and of itself, can serve as the driving force for the community.

I believe this logic is fundamentally flawed. If you're a mustard company, my love for mustard simply isn't enough to keep me engaged in your community long enough to build my loyalty, regardless of what sort of community-building efforts you employ. I believe there's a more powerful way to bind your customers and cultivate stronger customer community. For instance, when I'm connected to other mustard lovers, and we're able to discuss what mustards we've tasted, or how we've last used mustard, or what we're going to do with mustard tomorrow, then the community starts to form. It evolves because of human connection. The secret is to put the right tools and systems in place to allow those shared interests, values, and beliefs to spread from one member of the community to another.

Step Four: Let Go to Grow

Remember when I said that the best communities are insular and present an "us vs. them" mentality while also being open and welcoming to those who are new? Communities aren't always meant to be corporate-owned structures where the conversation is dictated and controlled. They are meant to grow organically and every aspect (from discussions to levels of participation) should be allowed to grow organically as well. Communities should be dynamic and shaped by your customers—not by you.

Here's an example: Earlier this year when I purchased a new Audi Q5 SUV, I found myself with a couple of questions not answered in the owner's manual. A quick Google search led me to AudiWorld.com, a private community created and operated by Audi aficionados. As of this writing, the site had 277,890 members, 23 million individual posts, and more than 2.7 million discussion topics. Even if Audi wanted to, it probably couldn't create a community like this. Well, in any event, it would be challenging. But that's okay. A forum that isn't created by your organization carries a more powerful level of authenticity than one that is. If your company gets to a point where your customers are creating their own forums to discuss your products and services in a positive way, then congrats! You've discovered the Holy Grail of online community building.

Some corporate entities would run to legal to try and have everything shut down. This is a control issue. But more important than having ultimate control is understanding that when loyalty to your brand has grown to a point where customer evangelists have taken it upon themselves to encourage participation and discussion—about you and without you—have the courage to let them run with it. Sometimes, you have to let go to grow.

The same phenomenon has happened with companies such as Jeep, Dell, and Disney. Letting go can be scary and daunting, but it represents one of the most powerful aspects of community growth. Don't dictate; participate. Your community will be built by real people with real human emotions. This undoubtedly means that disagreements will occur, and tempers will flare. It's to be expected; your goal is to do your best to keep things civil—and trust the process.

CHAPTER 5

Examining the
Principle of Content

The Beauty of Having a Multitude of Branches

While most kids were watching *The Flintstones* or *The Jetsons*, Steve Ells was watching Julia Child's *The French Chef*. Years later, when he graduated from college, he wasn't sure what he wanted to do with his life, but Child's unforgettable voice still lingered in his head, and Ells was sure he was passionate about food. He decided to follow that passion and enrolled at the Culinary Institute of America. After graduating, he moved to San Francisco to work at the famed Stars restaurant.

One day, while visiting a small *taqueria* in San Francisco's Mission District, Ells bit into a burrito and had a vision: Could a simple and relatively quick item like a burrito be transformed into something even more unique?

Ells decided to act on this vision. He found a small building and, with help from his dad to the tune of an $85,000 loan and equity purchase, Ells launched his first casual restaurant. Unlike other fast-food joints, Ells's establishment featured super-fresh produce, meats that came from animals raised naturally (without the use of hormones or antibiotics), and a unique customer experience that allowed patrons to create their own individualized burrito—starting with a fresh tortilla and working their way through a wide selection of ingredients, ending with different salsas. Sound familiar? This was the birth of Chipotle.

Chipotle doesn't just sell burritos; it offers a magnificent customer experience—one that's been carefully crafted and cultivated over the years. A page on Chipotle's website describes the vision: "It takes more than great tasting food to make a terrific meal. It takes an awesome location and eating with fun, interesting people. Unfortunately we can't make your friends any more interesting or fun. What we can do is carefully design each of our restaurants to create a unique dining experience fundamentally different than you would get with traditional fast food."[1]

Ells gets it. He understands that Chipotle's success derives from more than just the food (the content) it offers. He knew from an early stage that his restaurant needed to embrace the character of the company he wanted to build as well as the community he wanted to build it for. Chipotle's success has been nothing short of remarkable. What started with a single store, a single vision, and a loan from Dad has grown into a company with more than 1,595 stores and revenues of $3.21 billion. Chipotle is Evergreen![2]

This is the principle of content.

WHAT, EXACTLY, IS "CONTENT"?

The word *content* is commonly used by most marketers to describe the material that a company generates to discuss its products and services. Think blog posts, tweets, articles, and books. This is the "content" most people are familiar with. In my utmost humble opinion, however, in this day and age the word *content* should be used in a more expansive manner to describe the products you sell, the services you offer, or the information you create. In other words, content is what your company does or provides for your customers. But, more than that, content refers to all exchanges of value in the digital era. And in that sense, content is less about the actual physical manifestation of what you do and more closely related to the experience you provide. Confused? It may take a little while for this concept to fully sink in, so read on.

Many organizations believe what they do is the most important component of their success. They get caught up in their core product or service offering and pay little attention to the things that matter most—mainly the customers' experience and the feelings they associate with doing business with the company. The principle of content is about offering your products and services in a way that best compliments your character and community, and it's about finding the best ways to serve your existing customer base, without resorting to continuously trying to come up with the Next Best Thing guaranteed to entice new customers.

For decades, organizations found their competitive advantage through low product pricing, high product quality, and strong customer service. But recently, the model has shifted. Now the best and most profitable organizations find their competitive advantage by providing a compelling and emotionally engaged customer experience. Consider a company like Dell, for example. Dell realizes that its content needs to be great, but in this day and age, that alone is not enough. That's why Dell invites its customers to "Build It Yourself." Each person is able to specify the various components of his or her computer, customizing it to meet specific desires. Dell recognizes that this creation experience provides a heightened level of attachment to the content that goes beyond what the customer actually gets once the computer is delivered. The computer itself ultimately has meaning beyond being a simple commodity; the business process itself creates an emotional attachment with the object. Is the principle of content starting to make sense now?

You might, at first, find yourself reluctant to use the word *content* to describe your company's products and services—and, especially, to describe an emotionally engaged customer experience. But the Internet has changed the world. There's no denying that. And we'll continue to see it change the world—in ways we've never imagined. The rise of mobile phones has dramatically increased our interconnectedness. It has also changed our posture; we have become people who walk around hunched over as we stare at our phones. While on our phones (or on our computers) we are constantly engaged in content, much of that related to products and services we're purchasing. But is content really just marketing collateral—often referred to as "content marketing"—just simply the information used to sell our products and services? Or has content shifted into something bigger and something more profound than how we're currently looking at it? I tend to think the latter.

WHY IS CONTENT SO IMPORTANT?

Your company's content (what you do and the *value* that you provide) may be enough for you to sustain and survive, but your products, services, or information alone won't allow your organization to thrive. It certainly is not enough to engage customers in a way that they're likely to become raving customers. As this massive digital and mobile shift has occurred worldwide, your content has becomes less important to everything else your organization does. Surprised? You shouldn't be. Customers still want a high-quality product or service that both meets and exceeds their expectations. Yet at the same time they are silently begging for so much more. They are silently begging for brands to create products and services that meet deeper emotional and psychological needs.

Organizations haven't been forced to meet these new needs before, but now we have no choice. Even the smallest of businesses needs to do more. Consider your local Laundromat, for example. You drop off your clothes. The company performs a service. You pick up your clothes and go home. In short, the laundry service provides its content, and in exchange you provide remuneration. On the surface, there's little more to the equation. But I'll show you how even a small business like this, with very little human touch, can do so much more than just provide content. And when a company is able to do more, it sees increased customer retention, increased profits, and greater word-of-mouth referrals—and it starts to experience the many benefits of being Evergreen.

Understanding Your Content in Context

Take a look at the pyramid in Figure 5-1. It shows each of the Three Cs and how they function strategically in an Evergreen organization.

FIGURE 5-1

The Evergreen Triangle

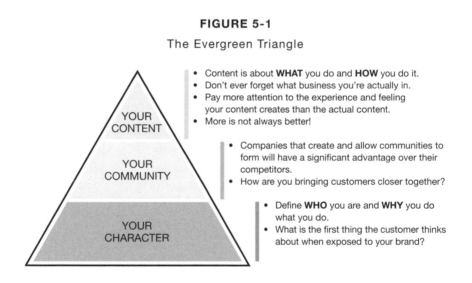

I can hear you now: "But, Noah, our products and services are what got us where we are today. They are the bedrock of our company. They belong at the bottom, right?" Most companies react this way. It's natural, given the business models we're used to looking at, but it's misguided. Most business models would suggest everything starts with your products and services, and you spread your wings from there, but I'm asking you to approach things differently. I'm also suggesting that this is a necessity if you want to grow in our increasingly connected world.

These days the most successful organizations understand that the content their customers buy is judged on the overall experience with the company. Products such as the iPod and iPad are unique, no doubt, but Apple clearly recognizes it wasn't the first company to have an MP3 player or a tablet device. Apple understands that the design and packaging of its content, the service provided at the point of sale, and the after-purchase support all impact the customer's lasting impression of the brand. The content itself is only one small part of the overall experience. Apple is also careful to fully understand its ideal customer archetypes, which I'll talk more about in Chapter 6.

Don't get me wrong—or misread the figure. Your company's content isn't less important than your character and community. Rather, it should be supported by your character and community. Your content is what generates a response. It's emotional. Content is about the benefit your products or services provide, or the way they make your customer feel. Content is *value*. Without great content, nothing is available to get the customer excited. Without content, nothing is available to solve a specific problem your customer might be experiencing. Your content changes lives and offers immense benefits. And, if you are willing to approach your content in a new way, it can become even more powerful.

Casting Off an Outdated Model

Most organizations don't really care enough about the customer experience. Why? Well, for a long time it wasn't how they maximized profits. Profits were maximized through the sale and delivery of products and services. Companies had a duty to their shareholders to do exactly that—sell and deliver products and services. Many companies still operate under this assumption, and rightfully so, to an extent. However, this is an outdated model.

While today's companies still have a duty to their shareholders, the game has changed. More companies than ever are taking a progressive approach—recognizing that they need to use their content to support a far more engaging customer experience. Many organizations are quickly coming to realize that they no longer have a choice. It's no longer enough to let all your decisions be guided by the endless pursuit of profit maximization without careful consideration of your customers and their experience. Let this be your guide to maximizing profits, but also to generating a new level of loyalty to what you do at the same time. Want to really impress your shareholders? This is the way.

EVALUATING THE NEW CUSTOMER EXPERIENCE

Organizations are often clueless about the actual customer experience, let alone the creation of an emotionally engaged experience. Your content is one of the main reasons your customer decides to do business with you initially. It's the utility of value you provide. But what makes your customer come back? What creates an experience that lasts and resonates? Let's look at a unique example.

Learning from Uber

Taxis provide very basic content. Actually, the taxi experience itself hasn't changed much since the seventeenth century, when horse-drawn carriages, also known as hackney carriages, first took passengers to their desired destinations. Not that you need a lesson in hailing a cab, but here's how it has worked for the past 300 or so years: You see a taxi and you wave your hand; a car (usually yellow) pulls over; you tell the driver where you want to go; the car takes you from point A to point B. Simple and effective content. Normally, very little else happens. But in 2009, two serial entrepreneurs, Garrett Camp and Travis Kalanick, had an idea that would change the industry.

Camp and Kalanick launched Uber—a company based on a game-changing idea that really couldn't be simpler. Using an application on your mobile phone, you request a car, and moments later a black town car or SUV picks you up. Very similar to the taxi model described previously, you tell the driver where you want to go and the driver takes you there. The "cash" transaction happens behind the scenes. Your credit card is billed automatically, and you don't tip the driver. It's seamless, which creates a far more enjoyable experience for the customer—one that resonates. Uber's rapid growth is the direct result of creating an emotionally engaged experience that people want to talk about.

Let's take a behind-the-scenes look at Uber from an operational perspective. Camp and Kalanick realized that cities all over the world had these small armies of private limousines idling outside office buildings, hotels, and apartments at any given time, literally just waiting for passengers. Their stroke of genius was to create a way for people looking to get from point A to point B to contact these town cars. They did this by giving each driver a mobile phone with an app that automatically processes each customer's request, identifies the closest driver, and allows that driver to either accept or deny the pickup. (If the pickup is denied, the request then goes to the next-closest driver. And so on.) Brilliant!

In his classic book *The Innovator's Dilemma: When New Technologies Cause Great Firms to Fail*, Clayton M. Christensen coined the term "disruptive technologies" to describe a phenomenon where innovations in products or services (in other words, the content that the company provides) drastically change the way the market uses those products or services. Uber has disrupted the taxicab industry. The existing industry didn't see it coming, nor was it prepared for how quickly Uber would rise as a major threat to the entire industry. And, because the threat has been so severe, Uber has faced a slew of regulatory opposition in almost every city it's entered into.[3] Alas, Uber has pushed forward and gained incredible momentum. But I digress. Let's get back to the content.

In terms of the car service that Uber offers, what has really changed? Besides allowing the consumer to use a mobile application to "hail a cab," the content has remained the same. An automobile still moves a customer from point A to point B. There's no flying car. No teleportation device. Uber didn't drastically change the content; Uber simply changed the customer experience. Uber can now be found in more than thirty-four countries and more than ninety cities, and that number is increasing rapidly.

The main takeaway is this: Regardless of the industry you're in, you don't need to create disruption. If you want to build a competitive advantage in our new (insanely connected) world, you may not need to change your content, but you do need to change the experience. Are you starting to see why character and community are so important to this equation?

Hyperfocusing on the Content—a Common Pitfall

In the endless pursuit of perfection, many organizations fail to build Evergreen relationships simply because they are too focused on their content. Let's face a cold, hard fact right here, right now. If you're in business and succeeding up until this point, then you're providing products and services that, most likely, already overdeliver and exceed your customers' expectations. Congratulations!

Now ask yourself, how many organizations do you know that don't provide, at the very least, satisfying content? You simply can't expect to stay in business long if your content isn't up to par. Whatever you provide has to be the very best. And if you've made it this far, it most likely already is quite good. Don't you think it makes sense, then, for you to spend your time ensuring that your customer experience is far superior to what your competitors are supplying? Don't you think it makes sense to focus on articulating your company's character and building a community among your customers?

KNOWING WHAT BUSINESS YOU'RE IN

In his quintessential 1960 article written for the *Harvard Business Review*, titled "Marketing Myopia," Theodore Levitt suggests the decline of many industries has essentially been caused by a misguided focus on the core delivery of what they do, rather than whom they do it for. They focus on the content and leave everything else up to the customer. Levitt's primary example is the railroad business—a booming industry only years earlier—which found itself in serious trouble with the disruption caused by the automobile. Levitt suggests that the decline of railroads was caused by the fact that industry executives assumed they were in the railroad business—that is, their business was focused solely on the content they offered. Levitt argues that they missed the fact that they were really in the transportation business.

In 2004, the *Harvard Business Review* suggested that marketing myopia was the most influential idea in marketing in the past fifty years. That doesn't mean that everybody has gotten the memo, though—or, perhaps more appropriately stated, not everyone has read the memo. Much like many of Peter Drucker's ideas are overlooked by today's executives (although his books adorn their shelves), so were many of Levitt's. However, in the past few years, there has been a dramatic rise in organizations that are trying to understand how customer loyalty, customer experience, and customer-centric focus can improve their operations.

That said, we need to be careful not to shift our entire strategic vision to one of only the customer, leaving our content to fend for itself. (It is possible for the pendulum to swing too far in the opposite direction, and that, too, would have disastrous consequences.) That's the reason I've positioned content as the third of the Three Cs. It represents both *what* you do and *how* you do it.

The key takeaway: More important than the core products or services that you offer is knowing what business you're actually in. Since you are reading this book, chances are good that you're in the marketing business (at least part of the time, if you wear multiple hats)—meaning that you have an opportunity to continuously create a customer experience that supports your content. Most restaurants, whether they know it or not, are in the experience business and rarely in the food business. Most boot companies are in the fashion business, not the footwear business.

Furthermore, sometimes you need to be nimble and shift course in defining which business you're in. With the disruption caused by advances in digital technologies, Kodak realized that it was no longer in the film business or even in the photography business, but that if the company wanted to survive (and thrive) it needed to position itself in the business of capturing and preserving memories. I hope this is making sense to you now. Don't confuse your content with what business you're really in.

KEEPING FOCUSED ON WHY
YOU DO WHAT YOU DO

Here's another simple truth about content: In today's world, it's more about the why than the *what*. Simon Sinek is right. We need to start with the why, but simply figuring it out isn't enough anymore. We need to take the why a number of steps further.

Now this is surprising to many people, largely because there was a time when it really was primarily about the what (and the why was a distant and distinctly secondary concern). In 1908, when Henry Ford introduced the Model T, it was really about the *what*. The Model T was new! It had a steering wheel on the left-hand side; the engine and transmission were enclosed; the four cylinders were cast in a solid block; the suspension used two semi-elliptic springs. It was simple to drive, and it was cheap. This was a car that everyone could afford. That's *what* it was. (Ford's empire took off, by the way, when he also focused on the *why*. Ford wasn't in the car business. He was in the personal independence and freedom business. But that's another story.)

Today, it is apparent that value, connection, and feeling have become more important factors than the content itself. Customers want more than just your content. They want to have an emotionally engaging experience with your company that makes them feel good. They want their intrinsic desires not only to be met, but to be exceeded. They want results and a specific outcome. This is the true meaning of value. *Value* is a term that's often misunderstood in business. *Value* is the result or outcome that customers receive when they do business with you. Indeed. But more than that, value is the feeling they get during the process. This seismic shift has changed, and is continuously changing, the face of doing business as we know it.

KNOWING WHEN MORE CONTENT IS BETTER—AND WHEN IT'S NOT

Let's talk about another fallacy related to content—that giving more intrinsically adds value to the customer experience. Furthermore, you may think that the more content you give, the happier your customers will be, and the more likely they will be to continue doing business with you. Let me tell you, this is a common misconception. Not only that, but it's one that, when put into practice, can seriously backfire. I've seen it happen. Many times. One of the critical details to establish about your company in regard to content is figuring out when less is more and when more is truly more—and knowing how to tell the difference.

Why Less Is Often More—Both for the Customer and You

Why would too much content be harmful when it comes to keeping customers and helping us build stronger relationships with those customers? We've all heard that bigger is better and more is better. And we know that customers want a bang for their buck. After all, there's nothing like a good deal, right?

Many companies respond to this impulse and say things like, "If we give our customer this much *stuff*, why on earth would they ever stop doing business with us? They will absolutely love how much *value* we give!" I hear variations on this statement all the time, especially from online service providers that are offering memberships, software services, and online tools.

This is a mistake. Too much choice and too many selections cause our customers to feel inundated. Too many e-mails and suddenly they're feeling overwhelmed. Too much, too fast, and before we know it they're looking for a way to stop doing business with us. All the while we are often thinking, *There's no way our customers will leave with this much THUD factor.* But our customers are often thinking, *I'm never going to use all this stuff. I'll come back later when I have more time.* Or they are thinking, *Too many e-mails! Leave me alone!* Or some variation thereof.

In short, we've missed an opportunity. A prospective customer hasn't connected with our brand because we've relied solely on our (abundant) content as a means to motivate that person to do business with us. The real problem with this scenario is that we were so busy adding content that we forgot to consider the other two of the Three Cs.

If your organization is guilty of this, I have good news. By implementing and taking the other two Cs (character and community) seriously, you'll reduce costs because you'll be less likely to overdeliver on your content; in turn, customers will be thrilled about doing business with you because you are actually, in effect, giving them more by giving them less. Yes, I'm giving you permission to deliver less content. But, *no*, that doesn't mean the local restaurant can start giving half its normal serving of food. And, no, the barber cannot cut half your hair. Not at all. It simply means—to reiterate what I said earlier—that content is a necessary but insufficient prerequisite for the ongoing and future success of your organization. Related to this idea is the importance of presentation, which brings us to ...

The Messy Closet Theory

Buying a vehicle is hard work. There's nothing easy about it. Today we can literally choose from hundreds of makes and models—not to mention countless variations of colors, options, and safety features—many of which change with each passing year. It can be one of the most challenging buying experiences on the planet. Entire magazines are dedicated to helping us choose the right SUV, the perfect luxury car, or the top budget minivan. On the one hand, we welcome the ability to customize and build our own vehicles based on personal tastes or budgets. On the other hand, the sheer number of choices is daunting, which is why some customers simply shut down during the selection process.

Take, for instance, my father-in-law, who bought a new truck a few years ago. He can be a little particular. He knows what he wants and knows what he likes. When he went to the dealership and asked for a truck with no stereo, eyebrows were raised. "You mean you don't want satellite radio? Just a CD player?" No, he meant he just wanted a plain-Jane AM/FM radio. Then he explained to the sales rep that he wanted a manual transmission and *didn't* want power windows.

In short, my father-in-law wanted a truck that would have been considered "standard" circa 1975, back before we were able to customize our selections ad infinitum. Personally, I think he would have kept my mother-in-law slightly happier on a recent 5,000-plus-mile trek across North America to see the majestic Sequoia National Forest if he had opted for air-conditioning. But he refused to engage with the customization process. It was all just too overwhelming. In the end, he was indeed able to get exactly what he wanted—though I think he actually paid *more* to have certain (now-standard) features taken away.

My father-in-law's actions can be explained beautifully by the Messy Closet Theory, which goes something like this: Too much content can quickly lead to an impression akin to encountering a messy closet. And who enjoys that? A messy closet makes it impossible to know what choices you have, what you want, and what goes together. It is impossible to think in a messy closet. Customers who feel as though they have just walked into a messy closet are generally overwhelmed by the experience and often simply turn around and run for the hills. In fact, having a "messy closet," is one of the primary reasons a business loses its existing customers.

In short, more is not always better. We've been led to believe that continuously adding new content can positively impact customer retention and loyalty. But it's a lie, and we, as business professionals and marketers, need to resist the temptation to add more. These days, our customers are inundated with choice and selection in their daily lives. Adding more during their experience with your company can, at best, slow down the buying process and, at worst, turn your customers away altogether.

Are you putting your customers into a messy closet, or is your customer experience as clean, efficient, and user-friendly as it could be?

When More Content Is, in Fact, Better

This is not to say that choices and options aren't important. In fact, sometimes nuanced choices are essential—but only when they deliberately tie back to the content and are specifically designed with the character of the target consumer in mind. For instance, I have a friend who drives a Bentley. It's a $250,000 car. When I nudged him about the cost of this incredible machine, he explained to me that the car is almost 100 percent custom. He and his wife spent months contemplating the various options for both the exterior and interior components. They labored for days over the color of the interior leather and the threading, which holds it together. In bed at night they would flip through brochures and talk about veneer. Would they choose chestnut, bird's-eye maple, or maybe piano black? They loved the entire six-month-long process. The decision-making process created a sense of excitement, and they anxiously anticipated the car's creation. It was a wonderful, emotionally engaged experience that we can learn from. Tremendous value can be derived by your customers' experience of the content before they even have the actual content. Pretty cool, right?

This exceptionally hands-on buying process works beautifully for Bentley. After all, Bentley carefully tailors its selections to its ideal customer. Bentley knows what kind of experience most of its customers want—and it goes to great lengths to enhance that experience at each step of the buying process. Bentley buyers are discerning about the details and enjoy the selection process. If your company's content profile is similar to Bentley's, by all means indulge your customers with lavish choices. But if you find yourself adding more content in the hopes of attracting more new customers, or keeping your existing ones, then you're more than likely simply adding confusion to the process. Try another approach.

Learning from Google

Remember a few paragraphs ago when I introduced the Messy Closet Theory? Well, here's a helpful visual that will allow you to digest what we've been talking about and take it a step further: Imagine that every piece of clothing owned by everybody who lives in your house was dumped unceremoniously into a single closet, with no rhyme or reason. Every morning before leaving for work, you would have to sort through this random collection. Trying to find a specific piece of clothing would become a ridiculous chore. Looking for your favorite red sweater? Keep digging.

Google took the world's largest messy closet and added one single thing: organization. Google understands that, more than anything else, what matters is organization and easy, reliable access to what you need. Why do you think Google's home page is a single box? It is immediately clear that you should type something into the box, and Google will show you where to find information about that topic.

Search engine optimization specialists spend their days trying to keep up with Google's continuously changing search algorithms. These specialists might help a client reach the coveted number one spot on Google through various manipulations, linkings, and other tactics. But that client might drop out of sight (and out of mind) when Google updates its search algorithms. What exactly is Google doing—and why? Well, very simply, Google is making it easier for you to find exactly what you want, and quickly.

Learning from Dropbox

One of my favorite examples of a company that gets it right is Dropbox, a free website that lets you easily share, store, and sync your documents, photos, and videos across multiple computers. On the home page you'll find four links. That's it. Four buttons you can press. Don't know what Dropbox is? Learn more. (Click here.) Ready to join? Sign up. (Click here.) Download Dropbox. (Click here.) Already a member? Sign in. (Click here.)

Dropbox couldn't make the customer experience any more idiot-proof. (There's a lot to be said about the term "idiot-proof," but I digress; that's a discussion for another day.) Dropbox isn't dillydallying around trying to convince you that this is the latest and greatest tech tool since sliced bread; instead, it cuts to the chase. The company focuses on offering a great customer experience based on the simplicity of the content. Could Dropbox add various bells, whistles, and features? Sure, but that would dilute the content. I chose a website's brilliantly designed user interface to make my point, but—whether your company is a retail establishment, restaurant, or any other business, for that matter—the basic advice is the same.

Customers appreciate choice. Don't get me wrong. What customers *don't* appreciate is choice at the expense of the customer experience. They don't appreciate an experience that becomes difficult because they are faced with too many choices. All too often, companies use choice as a crutch—a crutch that distracts us from creating better, more interesting, more appropriate experiences for our customers. Instead of asking yourself how you can give your customers more content, ask yourself how you can tidy up the content and make the customer experience more enjoyable.

You should also be asking how you can make it easier for your customers to buy from you. For example, are your invoices as easy to understand as they should be? Is your website experience optimized as efficiently as possible for customers to complete their desired tasks? Is calling your support line a straightforward process, or does the customer need to sort through piles and piles of clothes before reaching a human? You get the idea.

THE EVERGREEN DIAGNOSTIC

What type of company is yours? What type of business do you have? In this next section I'm going to share with you one of my favorite ways of showing business leaders how to understand what type of relationship they have with their customers and why a primary focus on content may be destroying their business.

One of the main comments I hear from clients is: "Noah, our company is different. We're merely a transactional business and don't have an opportunity to really engage the customer." I don't mean to be a spoiler, but most business transactions are just that—transactions. We give our customers content, they give us money, and the exchange is complete. It's business as usual, and we've been told that as long as we provide great service, the rest will take care of itself.

Let me tell you, the rest *very rarely* takes care of itself. Your content may meet your customers' basics needs and desires, and they may be mostly satisfied by the transaction. But who wants to run a business based merely on satisfaction? This scenario creates many lost opportunities on multiple levels, and it's up to you to take action if you want to increase sales and profits.

I've developed the Evergreen Diagnostic, shown in Figure 5-2, which features distinct quadrants representing each of the four different types of companies (starting with the upper-left and journeying counterclockwise): Deciduous, Barren, Wilting, and Evergreen. A company is posi-

FIGURE 5-2

The Evergreen Diagnostic

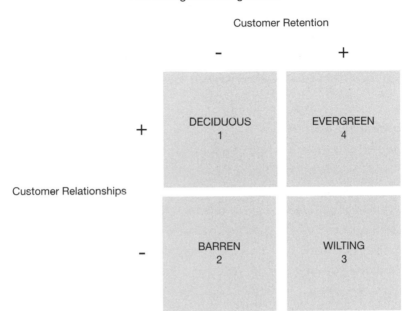

Customer Retention

	−	+

Customer Relationships

+

DECIDUOUS
1

EVERGREEN
4

−

BARREN
2

WILTING
3

tioned in one of the quadrants based upon two criteria—how well it nurtures customer relationships (or not, as the case may be) and how successfully (or not) it retains existing customers. Read through the narratives that follow, and then ask yourself which description best reflects your company.

Quadrant 1: Deciduous

Most companies, surprisingly, reside in the Deciduous quadrant. (I'd guess about 40 percent.) They operate with the intent to build great relationships with their customers and provide a high level of service. However, for one reason or another (such as the story I told about my bank in Chapter 1), this plan doesn't fully materialize and, as a result, they are unable to retain their customers. Like deciduous trees, these companies lose many leaves (customers) each year and therefore need to "grow" new ones. This type of business has its ups and downs, but winter is always cold, with no leaves on the tree. Deciduous companies end up constantly playing the cat-and-mouse game of customer acquisition, and the new customer addiction often proves too strong to break. This is what the status quo looks like. Is your company Deciduous?

Quadrant 2: Barren

Many organizations operate like barren trees, incapable of bearing fruit (or sustaining leaves). In fact, probably 30 percent of organizations today exist in this category. There is no customer relationship, and because of that, there's no longevity to the relationship. These companies exist in a state similar to Dr. Seuss's Waiting Place in *Oh, the Places You'll Go*, only applicable to businesses. They are just kind of stuck. Companies can survive in the Barren quadrant, based on a high investment in advertising and marketing that generates a continuous stream of transactions from new customers, but it's a challenging place from which to do business.

Quadrant 3: Wilting

Many organizations operate like a wilting tree—the leaves hang on, but they do not receive adequate sustenance from the tree and therefore are not as healthy as they should be. This kind of company is able to retain its customers, but there's no real relationship—or any attempt to create one. (Probably about 20 percent of businesses today fall in this category.) Classically, the insurance industry used to fall into the Wilting quadrant. On balance, insurance companies had high customer retention, but they did very little to make their customers feel as though they truly cared about keeping them around. (This business model, by the way, has been flipped on its head in recent years, since the Internet has made it easier for people to simply pack up and move to a new provider.) One downside of being a Wilting business is that since there is no customer relationship, the business fails to reap the benefits of positive word-of-mouth marketing and ongoing referrals. At the same time, customers of Wilting companies often exaggerate negative experiences and spread unflattering comments when things don't go as planned. Because these bad habits are often deeply ingrained, it can be very difficult to go from Wilting to Evergreen.

Quadrant 4: Evergreen

An organization that has great relationships with its customer base will experience greater customer longevity and retention of those customers. In turn, these companies live a long and fruitful life. They are not just focused on building a wonderful relationship with each customer, but they are also strategically focused on keeping customers coming back. They're also focused on increasing referrals and creating customer communities. They understand the true value of a customer and focus on keeping customers engaged and active. They have tactical retention and reactivation systems in place to keep customers coming back again, and again, and again. This is what it means to be Evergreen. About 10 percent of organizations get it right all the time. Don't worry—I can lead you to the promised land.

GOING BEYOND "THE TRANSACTION"

It doesn't matter what type of company you consider yours to be. What matters is that you are committed to moving out of your existing quadrant and into the Evergreen quadrant. So you might be asking what this has to do with your products and services. Well, I hope by now you recognize that what you provide in terms of content is far less important than *how* you provide it—and furthermore, that *no matter what business you're in*, your company can benefit from focusing on the customer experience.

To prove my point, let's consider tires for a minute—or, more precisely, how a tire company can build customer loyalty and maximize customer value. Perhaps you're thinking, *Noah, have you lost your mind? After all, isn't every tire company the same?* Absolutely not! Believe me. Some tire companies have taken the steps necessary to build Evergreen customer relationships, and they are thriving. They have done it by strategically moving their business toward the Evergreen quadrant. Their content didn't change; they simply changed the customer experience. They switched from providing one-stop transactions, or simply selling a commodity, to creating emotionally engaging experiences.

You're thinking: *An emotionally engaged experience buying tires? How do you do that?* Well, these companies are very clear about their character and they have created structures of community. Yes, it's true. Even a tire company can have an effective monthly newsletter, or an active Facebook profile, or the structures for customer communities to form.

Consider a company such as Belle Tire, which is based in Allen Park, Michigan. With almost 4,000 Facebook fans, 3,500 Twitter followers, and a very active blog, this business is actively engaging its clients in an experience that goes far beyond just "I need new tires." Online, Belle Tire invites its customers to participate in a wide range of discussions— from tires to (the Detroit) Tigers. In addition, the company blogs on a number of different yet highly relevant topics, such as car care, driving safety, and how to save on holiday road trips. It even publicly deals with any less-than-favorable customer experiences in an open, honest, and authentic fashion. Belle Tire is also actively involved in the local community, supporting schools, sponsoring youth hockey clubs, and donating to other nonprofit organizations. If a tire company can do it this well, then there's no reason why your organization can't be doing it, too.

Make no mistake. The concepts I'm sharing in this book aren't for one specific type of company. They can be embraced by organizations across a wide array of industries. Organizations are learning that they can both maximize customer value and build remarkable, loyal relationships with their customers at the same time.

Every time you engage in a transaction with a customer your business has an opportunity to go beyond the transaction. Your goal should not be to simply sell your content in exchange for money. Your goal should be to look at every transaction with a customer as a chance to create a long-term relationship with a tremendous amount of long-term value. Remember: Your character and your community are what truly support your content.

Think about how you want customers to interact with and remember your brand. Creating emotionally engaged experiences shouldn't be difficult. In fact, it can be downright easy and fun, yet most organizations continue to believe that customers come for their content. Customers *don't* come for the content. They come for an outcome, and that's really where value begins. And next, customers stay for the character and community—in short, the customer experience.

So how, exactly, do you go about building a dynamic customer experience? Remember the old cliché: "We provide *wow* service!" The problem with the "wow experience" is that everyone aspires to create one, but most are rather dull. They're dull because they're generic. The key to the power of the Three Cs is to effectively articulate *specific* things about your organization to create a more dynamic and engaging experience for the customers who do business with you. To be effective, your company's "*wow* experience" needs to resonate with your customer on a deep emotional level. It's too simple to say you need to create a *Cheers*-like atmosphere where everyone knows your name. In today's world, everyone knows everyone's name. You need to go above and beyond casual lip service.

To this end goal, I offer you this: The rest of the book will be far more tactical about how to put the Three Cs concept (and many more ideas) to work in your organization. I'll offer numerous tactics that are guaranteed to generate massive increases in profits. Get ready to fertilize the ground, in preparation for encouraging tremendous growth.

PART TWO

Fostering Growth

CHAPTER **6**

Becoming Intimately Familiar with Your Customers

Getting Your Hands in the Soil

Companies are struggling. As we've discussed, old sales and marketing methodologies rely on manipulations to generate sales, but that model clearly doesn't work anymore. Unfortunately, neither do a lot of the things that you may have read (or been taught) when you were coming up the ranks. For instance, anyone who has spent any time at all in marketing has heard about the Four Ps—product, price, place, and promotion. These concepts were made leading edge by marketing professor Philip Kotler in his 1967 book, *Principles of Marketing*, and they ruled the roost for more than forty-five years. But the game has changed, and, unfortunately, the Four Ps are now dead.

In the early 1990s, Robert Lauterborn, a widely recognized and influential professor at the University of North Carolina, proposed a reclassification of the Four Ps (from a more customer-oriented perspective), suggesting that they might be better described as the Four Cs—customer, cost, convenience, and communication.[1] Kotler eventually agreed and accepted this position.[2] I greatly respect both of these influential leaders in the field of advertising and marketing, but I strongly believe there's an easier and far more effective path for marketers and business leaders. What really matters these days is your character, community, and content—the Three Cs.

It's a bit like alphabet soup—and it may be hard to digest. But, in short, the ongoing problem we routinely run into is that marketing is still viewed as a purely tactical endeavor focused on the "new customer addiction." These tactics are important, of course, but while many organizations are busy trying to make the perfect six-second Vine video—or get the right post on Twitter, a better picture on Instagram, or more likes on Facebook—their competitors are focused on more important endeavors, thereby increasing profits by 50 percent or more. Which would you rather spend your time on?

To thrive in business these days you need to shift your focus from approaching marketing as a tactical operation to approaching marketing as a more methodical, more strategic endeavor. Your marketing team shouldn't be spending months on creatives, wondering if the logo is placed just right or the font is perfect and properly justified. Yet that's exactly what's consuming most of their time. And it's exactly why we have so much terrible marketing and so much misunderstanding about social media and other methods of communicating with our customers and prospects.

For years, Fortune 500 companies have gotten wrapped up in branding, and now they're getting equally wrapped up in how to do effective social media. If you are anything smaller than a Fortune 500 company, then you should be wrapped up in results. Your team should be focused on the Big (Strategic) Picture—getting the Three Cs right, thereby increasing customer value *and* increasing revenues. You might not realize it, but your marketing department may be the most important department in your entire organization. They're the ones focused on bringing customers in, and hopefully by now you recognize that they're also the ones in the driver's seat when it comes to keeping them. This chapter and, in fact, all the chapters in Part Two, are about strategic marketing and how to ensure your organization is focused with laser precision on the fastest, most effective marketing and business growth opportunities available to you. *Nothing* will change your business faster and better than more powerful marketing.

When a Kevlar bulletproof vest is made, dozens of layers of tightly woven fabric are interlaced together. Layer upon layer upon layer. This chapter, and the five that follow, contain actionable concepts that serve as your layers of Kevlar fabric. Your job is to interlace the layers—with each other, as well as within your organization. Successfully doing so will create marketing results that are nearly bulletproof. You'll be able to implement processes and procedures to help retain customers, increase transactions, and build greater Evergreen loyalty.

Now that you understand the Three Cs in theory, let's discuss specific ways to put these ideas into practice—starting with how to establish a better understanding of your customer.

WHY CUSTOMER LIFETIME VALUE IS BROKEN—AND HOW TO FIX IT

In Chapter 1, I explained that the biggest faux pas many organizations make when it comes to understanding customer lifetime value (CLV) is that they view their customer base as a single amorphous entity and use an "average" of the data they've collected to make their most pressing and important business decisions. Furthermore, they communicate with their customers as this single entity, as if "one message fits all." Unfortunately, this type of thinking is wrong, and it's both costing a lot of money and causing a lot of undue stress. It's also what's at the core of very bad marketing—and there's a lot of it out there these days.

Even though I touched on this subject briefly in Chapter 1, let's take a more in-depth look at this traditional model—what it is, exactly, and why it doesn't work very well anymore—and then take a peek at a few things we can work on to fix it.

Calculating Your Company's CLV

Despite all the drawbacks and negative aspects of traditional CLV calculations, knowing the CLV number across your entire base of customers is still one of the most important insights you can ever have about your business. Therefore, you really should learn how to do this calculation the "old school" way. Figuring out your organization's CLV is simple. In the most basic sense, you take all the profit from your client base, determine how long these customers have done business with you (on average), subtract all the advertising, marketing, and other costs associated with servicing that customer, and—voilà—you have your CLV number.

Hundreds, if not thousands, of calculators are available online that will allow you to punch in numbers to learn your average CLV. Some of these tools are basic and some far more complex, and I don't want to reinvent the wheel here. You might already have an incredible team of marketers and data analysts who can quickly tell you your CLV with a degree of certainty. If not, I would suggest you simply Google "CLV" and use one of those tools. But keep in mind, this method is fraught with pitfalls.

Defining What "Lifetime" Really Means

One of the biggest and most glaring issues should be obvious to you. It's the question of lifetime. In regard to customer lifetime value, who determines what the "lifetime" of a customer really is? It isn't really a lifetime (in other words, the span between a customer's birth and death), is it? If it's not, then is it sixty days, three months, two years, or a decade? The problem is we don't really know. Furthermore, do we really have to wait a lifetime to determine an accurate number for our CLV? If so, good luck.

Each business needs to determine what its specific "lifetime" is—for a number of reasons. Namely, having a defined lifetime will let you know when a customer is no longer actually a customer. (Is a customer who bought something from you three years ago still a customer, for instance?) I'll discuss this topic at length in Chapter 10, since it makes people in many organizations scratch their heads. But, in brief, do you think that customer should be marketed to and communicated with in the same way you communicate with a customer who just purchased from you last week? Of course not! But guess what most organizations are doing? Hmmm... Are *you* guilty?

Instead of focusing on a single number for CLV, consider first the importance of understanding the makeup of your customer base; then determine lifetime value based on that information and a number of other criteria. Read on!

Taking Issue with the Word *Average*

Just like the word *lifetime* can create stumbling blocks if we're not careful, we also have to be truthful about the fact that—and I don't care *what* business you are in—there is no such thing as an "average customer." You have different groups of customers, which we'll discuss soon, all of whom deserve your unique attention. For example, you might have a segment of grandmothers and a segment of teenagers, each requiring very different marketing and messaging. Or you might have a group of customers that spans from, say, executives to assembly-line workers. Can you see why having one single database (and one single CLV number) can create such a huge problem and ineffective marketing? Every day organizations calculate fancy variations of their CLV numbers, but it's no wonder that so many of them don't know how to use this data effectively to increase their profitability.

In Chapter 3, when I introduced the principle of character, I only talked about how this concept pertains to your organization. But that's only half of its potential application. Later in this chapter I'm going to focus on how you can articulate the character of your customer base. This is an absolutely critical factor that determines whether (or not) you are able to effectively engage and communicate with current and prospective clients. The important thing to understand about your customer base is that you don't just have a single ("average") customer profile.

Understanding Who Your Customers Are— and What They Are Doing

Traditional marketing typically focuses on two distinct types of profiles and datasets for customers. One is based on the demographics and characteristics of an organization's customers; the other is based on activity and how the customer consumes (or uses or derives value from) the company's content. As an example of the former, the demographic profile, a manager might claim: "Our average customer is female, 37 years old, married, has two kids, and makes $75K per year." As an example of the latter, when I work with online entities to boost retention, I typically help them look at behavioral and activity-based data. We focus on how customers are behaving. What are they doing after the purchase? How often are they logging onto a website, for example, or posting a comment? How often are they submitting support requests? Did they sign up and then not come back for three weeks? How many files do they download? How many pages do they visit? These are the types of questions we would look at in a Web environment. Similar questions, of course, can be created for almost any organization.

When a company focuses on behavioral analytics, its marketing staff looks at customers' consumption, usage, and participation levels, and then sorts the customers into different groups. This process can reveal incredibly valuable information, but the most powerful customer profile is one that defines characteristics and demographics while maintaining a watchful eye on behavior. Only when both types of data are combined together into one cohesive unit is a company able to recognize *who* its customers are and *how* they're behaving, thereby dramatically increasing the company's chances of communicating with its customers in a way that resonates.

Most organizations have a database of customers. Furthermore, most companies engage in traditional marketing (which involves, among other things, sending e-mails and engaging in social media). But most also make the mistake of blasting every person the same message. Everyone gets the same e-mail. Everyone gets the same promotion. Everyone gets the same update. Surely, there's got to be a better way to communicate. There is! And it starts with knowing, precisely, who your customers are.

CREATING YOUR IDEAL
CUSTOMER ARCHETYPES

In Chapter 3 you defined your corporate character. Now it's time to take the essence of that idea and shift your focus to your customer, with two important distinctions. First, when you create your corporate character, you create *one* character; when you create your ideal customer archetypes, you create *several*, with each being based on a distinct segment or group of customers. Second, your ideal customer archetypes are drawn from both demographic and psychographic traits of actual customers. This process is tremendously valuable, since it helps to define both the type of people you are trying to attract as a company and the people you're communicating with.

What, Exactly, Is an "Archetype"?

In the early twentieth century, Swiss psychiatrist and psychotherapist Carl Jung introduced the term *archetypes* in his work to describe the human psyche. He believed that all people could be categorized according to their individual archetype. Jung originally wrote about four distinct archetypes in his book *Die Struktur der Seele* (*The Structure of the Psyche*).

Almost a hundred years later, Dr. Carol S. Pearson expanded upon Jung's concepts and classified twelve different archetypes, making Jung's theories accessible to everyone. She includes the Innocent, the Orphan, the Warrior, the Caregiver, the Seeker, the Destroyer, the Lover, the Creator, the Ruler, the Magician, the Sage, and the Jester.[3] Pearson describes each archetype based on a number of different personality traits. For example, the Jester is the type of person who believes you only live once. The Jester's core desire is to live in the moment. This archetype's greatest fear is being bored (or worse, being boring to others). The Jester's biggest pitfall is wasting a lot of time, but hey, you only live once! Whereas, the Caregiver is more interested in the good of others. This archetype's core desire is to connect with and help others in life through selfless actions. The biggest fear of the Caregiver is being selfish and ungrateful. The Caregiver's greatest pitfall is being taken advantage of. The Caregiver is motivated by compassion and generosity.

Companies, too, can be categorized by archetype. In a book on that very topic, *The Hero and the Outlaw: Building Extraordinary Brands Through the Power of Archetypes*, authors Margaret Mark and Carol S. Pearson classify well-known companies according to the twelve personality archetypes. For example, Ben & Jerry's, the ice-cream company, is the Jester—a company that likes to have a good time. Whereas companies like Lego, Crayola, or GoldieBlox are Creators—companies interested in creating things of value. Thinking about your company as an archetype can be helpful while creating your character and defining why you do what you do, and how you conduct yourself.

And How Does This Concept Apply to Your Customers?

Even if this is the first time you've heard of Carl Jung and his archetypes, or Pearson's work, you surely already know, based on life experience, that everyone is different. Everyone interprets messages differently. Everyone reacts to things in his or her own unique way. And yet, so many companies are guilty of treating their customers as a single entity, speaking to everyone in the same manner. This is a huge mistake that can crush your business, and it's one of the primary reasons that many companies are terrible at marketing. Organizations must understand that marketing itself (as a discipline) and whom they are marketing to (the market) are two inextricably linked but distinct areas of focus. Instead of using a single CLV to communicate to nameless and faceless customers en masse, it is much more effective to have a library of your own company's customer archetypes and to communicate with each group of customers (and prospects) in an individual and authentic way.

Imagine for a moment the following scenario: A football game is being held in a giant stadium. Fans on one side of the stadium are dressed in one team's colors; it's a sea of red. On the opposite side are the opposing team's fans; it's a sea of yellow. As the game gets into full swing we clearly know which fans are rooting for which team. We know because of the color of the clothes they're wearing, the face painting, or who they're cheering for when one of the teams scores. Now empty the stadium and fill it with your customers and prospects. You might have two, four, or six groups. Every section of the stadium should be a different group, each wearing a different color. I'd like you, as referee, to call forward a captain from each group of customers for the coin toss. You should be able to, with relative precision, tell me what each person looks like as an individual. This is the archetype that represents that specific group of clients.

The main goal of this exercise is to paint a vivid picture of each segment of your customer base. However, if you find that you are having trouble describing each archetype, then your discovery process should start with selecting one group and asking a few simple questions, such as:

- If you could combine all the customers in this group and create a single person, who would it be?

- Is this person male or female?

- What does the person look like?

- Where does the person live?

- What is this person's income level?

- How old is the person?

- Is the person educated?

- What is this person's most burning desire?

- What are the person's goals and/or aspirations in life?

- What motivates this person?

- What is this person's biggest fear/pain/frustration?

- What goes through this person's head when waking in the morning?

- What does a "day in the life" of this person look like?

- What are the unique commonalities of the members of this particular customer group?

- What are their emotional hot-button issues?

- How do they communicate with each other?

- What makes this group of customers different from the other groups?

By no means is this an exhaustive list of questions. And feel free to tailor the list to suit your company's needs. The point of this exercise is simply to get you thinking about different groups of customers and fine-tuning the unique characteristics that make members of each group similar to one another. This process will inherently be easier for some companies than for others—particularly when organizations are fairly narrow in their appeal. But don't be lulled into oversimplifying your archetypes. Occasionally, a business will have a single customer archetype, and that's fine, but most businesses will have several.

It is worth noting that various incarnations of this idea are out there. In Keith Eades's 2003 book, *The New Selling Solution: The Revolutionary Sales Process That Is Changing the Way People Sell*, he refers to a similar process as creating your "straw man." Others have called it building your "customer avatar." Personally, I like to use the word *archetype* because most organizations have more than one ideal customer. Whatever you choose to call it, the concept is powerful when used strategically.

What Are the Benefits of This Approach?

Businesses love to talk about the "voice of the customer," but often these very same companies don't have a true understanding of the people they're actually talking to. How can we understand the customer's "voice" and what resonates with this person if we're not actually sure who the customer is? How can anyone possibly imagine this strategy will work, let alone foster loyalty to a brand? When organizations try to talk to everyone, they end up talking to no one.

When you take the time to learn about your ideal customer archetypes and build models to describe them, your organization becomes prepared to truly focus its marketing efforts. You know, intimately, who your customers are and how they behave. And it becomes crystal clear that each group of customers requires different marketing, different messaging, and different follow-up. You find yourself in the position of ensuring that all of your marketing efforts are speaking only to one type of person, which enables you to communicate without breaking rapport. Each customer, in turn, feels as though everything you do, or say, was created almost exclusively for him or her. It's as if you are generating thoughts already happening subconsciously in your customer's mind. This is when the magic happens.

To quote that tired old TV ad slogan: "But wait! There's more!" The benefits of creating models of your various archetypes go far, far beyond marketing. Archetypes can be used across your entire organization as a training tool. For example, they can give your customer service team members a better understanding of the type of person raising a complaint, and a clearer sense for how to communicate with that customer. They can also help your sales team members communicate more effectively with leads and more quickly identify new opportunities. In short, to get the most value out of this strategic approach, everyone in your organization should be fully versed in the archetypes of your ideal customers.

I'm sure you are starting to understand the potential ramifications of this concept. It's powerful stuff. But let's get back to marketing. Every time your organization communicates with either current or prospective customers, you need to ask yourself, "Will this message/marketing/copy/design resonate with *this* specific customer archetype?" Your ideal customer archetype should be the basis of every customer communication—before, during, and after the sale. If you follow this strategy systematically, you will generate the most effective marketing you've ever created; your organization will experience a major breakthrough. Guaranteed!

A Warning—Don't Let Predetermined Notions Hide Big Oceans

I once had a client who, after being in business for fifteen years, wasn't really sure who his ideal customers were. Well, to be fair, he had a general idea of what was unique about his customers. But he didn't have as deep an understanding of his customer profiles as he needed in order to maximize his company's potential. And he most certainly wasn't able to articulate his ideal customer archetypes. Sound familiar?

My client knew his customers were predominantly males age 40 and older. A good start, but the rest was mostly a guessing game. What made these men over forty tick? What was their driving motivation? What kept them up at night? What did they think about on the drive to work? We needed to find out.

We put forth a little effort to connect with and learn about his various customers, and to build archetypes for each of them. Within just a couple of sessions of working together, my client recognized he actually had three very distinct types of men who purchased his content, as follows:

- The first group consisted of men who were self-employed. They were nearly all married, most of them had kids, and they wanted to grow their companies. They were looking for marketing help to take their practices to the next level. Their biggest concern was that business growth had become somewhat stagnant.

- The second group were men in their sixties, also self-employed, who were wildly successful and now quickly edging toward retirement. They were mostly concerned with setting up their business to be sold in a couple of years or passed down to a family member. In a nutshell, they stayed awake at night thinking about what would happen to their businesses.

- The third group of men worked for larger manufacturing organizations. All were top-performing sales stars. These guys were mostly single, but some were married. That wasn't terribly important. What was important about this group was they all desired to start their own companies, and they needed the assistance and value from my client to help them do that.

Most companies would have considered the entire customer base as one type of customer. In this case, they would have said "our ideal buyer is a male age 40 and older." As such, most companies would send out one set of e-mails, engagements, sales processes, and promotions. However, this one-size-fits-all approach clearly would have overlooked crucial nuances—precisely the things that pinpoint areas of value just waiting to be mined.

The insights my client and I gathered allowed him to make some simple and subtle shifts in how he marketed his content to each group. Doing so, he said, was literally like "flicking a switch." His marketing results went from okay to amazing, and moving forward, this kind of smart, strategic marketing guided the organization to make better decisions about everything it did, across every department.

By segmenting his customers, my client was able to create three types of offers and promotions, three types of communications with customers—each with its own unique style and tone. He said results and response rates went through the roof on everything they did. Sales increased (both in terms of frequency and transaction size), and customers became far more loyal.

Are you guilty of treating all of your customers as one single entity? Just a little bit of extra work could drastically change your relationships with your customer base. Don't you think it's worth it?

COMMUNICATING WITH YOUR ARCHETYPES

For a long time, we, as marketers, have understood the importance of knowing our ideal client. However, up until now, very little effort has been focused on understanding our customers with the intent of building genuine, long-term relationships with them. In other words, thinking about archetypes from a customer retention standpoint. This is a quality reserved for Evergreen organizations—and with a little bit of effort that success can be yours. The only way to succeed is to not only have a better understanding of who those customers are, but to know how to communicate with them as well. Let's begin.

Step One: Get Inside Your Archetype's Head

If you really want to create effective marketing, you need to understand, on a visceral level, what it's like to be each individual archetype. To do this, you need to step inside this customer's head. This is how you learn about the customer's hot-button issues and what really makes that specific type of customer tick. Here are a few questions to get you started:

- What does a typical day in the life of your archetype look like?

- What fears or frustrations does your archetype deal with daily?

- What thoughts go through your archetype's mind?

- What keeps your archetype up at night?

- What does your archetype really want out of life?

- What motivates your archetype to keep going?

- What gets your archetype really excited?

- What challenges does your archetype face daily that might be holding this person back?

An aside: When I ask the first question, most people come to the sudden (*shocking!*) realization that their ideal customer doesn't spend all day thinking about their company. No, the customer is thinking about picking up the kids from school or getting an oil change, or wondering what's for dinner or if there's a line at the barber, or thinking about that toothache—hoping it doesn't require a root canal! But I digress.

Use these questions to build a profile that describes what a "day in the life" of each archetype looks like. They should provide a good starting point, but then flesh out the story by asking some additional questions: How does your content impact the life of your customer? How does it solve this customer's problem or meet a specific need or desire?

In his classic book *Crossing the Chasm: Marketing and Selling Disruptive Products to Mainstream Customers*, Geoffrey Moore claims that the way a company succeeds is by targeting a very specific group of customers and focusing all the company's resources on becoming the dominant leader in that specific marketplace. Moore worked with technology companies through a process of building a "day in the life of ..." their ideal customer. After a company had a pretty good idea of what that day looked like, he had company managers complete a second exercise where they created the day in the life of their ideal customer *after* he or she had used their product.

Think about your own content. If I asked you, right now, if you could describe what your customer's life was like before doing business with you and what it looked like afterward, could you describe the impact in detail?

Step Two: Understand Your Archetype's Voice

In Chapter 3, I asked you to imagine a fictional conversation between your ideal customer and your corporate character. Now that you're an expert on archetypes, I'd like you to imagine their conversation again. If they met for the first time today, what would they say to one another? How would they say it? Except there is a slight wrinkle in this new assignment. Now you know that you don't have just *one* ideal customer; you have multiple archetypes. And each of these individuals, of course, responds differently and communicates in a different manner. You need to try to capture each voice. To do this, ask yourself these questions:

- What specific words or phrases do each of your archetypes use?

- How would archetypes in specific groups talk to one another?

- Do they use sophisticated language? Or is their conversation more casual?

- Do your archetypes use shared lingo (recall the discussion on tribal lingo in Chapter 4), shorthand expressions, or acronyms?

Imagine if every time you communicated with your customers you acted as if you were having a face-to-face discussion with them. You're not talking to them, but rather you're conversing with them. This is how you should approach all of your messaging. Communicate on their level. Don't try to speak above your customers. Think about your own interactions. When people try to overpower you, overimpress you, or speak above you, you feel something is amiss. However, when people communicate with you in a genuine manner, rather than talk at you, the exchange engenders trust. You have the opportunity to create this type of feeling every time you communicate with your customers. Don't squander it!

As you are drafting your imaginary conversation, consider the overall tone of the specific archetype. For example, is your archetype casual or formal? We've been told during the past few years that we need to be more casual and real with our customers. But this advice is misguided, *if* it doesn't make sense to that specific archetype. You wouldn't want to be too casual if your customers were all retired brain surgeons. Similarly, you wouldn't want to be too computer techie if your audience was primarily senior citizens with very little computer experience. This is why it's important to recognize your various archetypes. Think of it like a cocktail party. What kind of cocktail party discussion would you have with this archetype outside of business hours? It may be casual, but not overly casual, or it may be a little more formal, depending on who is attending.

Step Three: Match Your Communication Plan with Each Group

When customers are connected to a company, and companies are connected to their customers, they understand each other's wants and aspirations and are able to relate on a deeper and more meaningful level. When a customer feels understood (particularly in a way that is as intimate as what we're talking about), then e-mails, messages, and everything else tend to resonate on a much deeper level. E-mails get opened. Messages have impact. Customers feel good about their relationship with your company, and they want to do business with you over and over and over again. Not only that. They want to identify themselves—and their own unique personalities—with your company's character.

So how do you get to this sweet spot? You need to understand your customers in a way that makes them much more real. You need to have a vision of your customer that's bigger and more clearly defined than how they actually see themselves.

Most organizations are obsessed with talking *at* people and not *to* them. By now, you are keenly aware that, to be successful in this day and age, you need to communicate with your customers personally. Instead of yelling from the mountaintop, you need to interact with your customers as though you are actually in a relationship with them. People don't want to do business with someone who talks at them; they want to do business with someone they like and can have a conversation with.

Remember Jamie Oliver's brand guidelines in Chapter 3? "Jamie is … approachable and fun—unpretentious, accessible, and playful," and so forth. While the guidelines don't identify who the ideal customers are, or which archetypes are identified, they do specify how the Jamie Oliver brand communicates with most people. Does how *you* currently communicate with your customers match the profile of the person you are trying to reach and, more important, the person you are trying to retain or build a relationship with? If not, then defining your customer archetypes in great detail can be a wonderful initiative for your company. These findings can have a dramatic impact on every facet of your organization—from the front lines to the executive suite.

Step Four: Be Only Where You Need to Be

Now it's time to start considering how—or, more specifically, *where*—you're going to communicate with your ideal archetypes. Here are a few sample questions to get you started:

- Do your ideal archetypes all use cell phones? Or do some of them still use fax machines?

- Are they plugged into social networks such as Twitter, Facebook, or LinkedIn? If not, how do they communicate with their friends or colleagues?

- Where do they hang out?

- Do they read books? If so, what type?

- How about traditional media sources? Do they read the newspaper, and if so, which one?

- Do they watch television? If so, what's their favorite thing to watch?

- What else is interesting or unique about them?

The purpose of these questions is to determine what marketing activities will align with your specific archetypes. This is, of course, not an exhaustive list. I'm simply giving you some questions to get you started, but I want you to ponder and dig as deep as you can. The more you know, the better position you'll be in. This is your opportunity to focus not just on where your current customers are, but also on where your prospects might be, and where they're likely to go. This is also your opportunity to articulate where you truly need to be, not where the social media experts tell you that you need to be.

So when the next hit start-up, "bamboozleboo.com," makes a big splash and everyone on the planet is in a mad rush to jump on the bamboozleboo train, you'll quickly recognize if it is a medium that your customers might use, if it's a place where prospective customers might hang out. (Or not!) Consequently, you'll instantly know if it makes sense for your company to focus its time, energy, and resources there. (Or not!)

I get e-mails all the time from companies that tell me they are doing everything on social media, but nothing's working. I visit their websites and see all the familiar logos: Like us on Facebook. Follow us on Twitter. View us on Pinterest ... Instagram, Vine, Flickr, YouTube, Snapchat, Tumblr, LinkedIn, Vimeo, RSS, and more! They're burnt out because they are trying to maintain profiles on all these social networks, or they're overpaying self-proclaimed social media experts to manage these important tasks for them (without a proper understanding of their corporate

character, which is crucial), and they're freaking out each time a new service gains critical mass and they're told they need to be there, too, or
they'll miss out on a great opportunity—the game-changing, be-all and
end-all opportunity for companies everywhere.

Stop it! Be only where you need to be.

The great Canadian former ice hockey player Wayne Gretzky once
said, "I skate to where the puck is going to be, not where it has been."
This doesn't mean you jump at every new opportunity or tech start-up.
Quite the contrary. It means you should get to the point where you have
such a grasp on your customer archetypes that you know exactly where
they are now, where they are going, and where they'll be next. That's the
type of insight "The Great One" applied to his hockey game, and it's the
same type of strategy you can apply to your marketing efforts. Focus.

CAPITALIZING ON THE NATURAL SYNERGY
OF THOUGHTFUL MARKETING

By now I'm sure it is crystal clear why the principle of character is so important—and why our discussion of the Three Cs started there. When a
company has gone to great lengths to define its character, and then takes
the next step to carefully define its different groups of customers, a lightbulb
goes on for the organization itself. Suddenly its marketing, its follow-up,
and its relationship building become a heck of a lot easier. When experts
talk about being "authentic," this is really what they're getting at.

We know that learning about our customer archetypes and the specific qualities that make up those customers allows us to market more
effectively, but it does more than that. It allows us to create a sense of
trust, faster. Loyalty isn't generated by the "*wow* experience." Loyalty is
generated by the feeling your customer gets from doing business with
your company.

But the magic doesn't stop there. Loyal customers tend to become
more active members of a company's community. And when that hap-

pens, suddenly a tremendously powerful synergy starts to occur—a synergy that has direct and measurable results. A synergy that points toward Evergreen.

As with anything in life, you want to be able to gauge progress and, more important, your return on investment. By shifting from a "new customer focus" to a "relationship-building focus," you will have time, energy, and money to spend on such things as community-building endeavors. To properly gauge your efforts, you need to be crystal clear on your strategies and objectives. From there, you should be able to devise the metrics to gauge your success. For example, if one of your objectives is for your community to help increase your referral business, then your marketing department must seek to measure how many new customers come to the community as a direct result of your community-driven initiatives.

Do you see the potential in this approach? It is a game changer, for sure. Are you willing to invest the time to learn more about your customers and, in so doing, gain their loyalty? If so, then you are primed and ready for Chapter 7. Read on.

CHAPTER 7

Getting Loyalty Programs Right

Building a Tree House and Letting
Your Customers Climb to Reach It

"I'll take three chicken burgers, four beef burgers, two pork chops, and half a pound of bacon." Not bad for a trip to the local butcher. The clerk asked me my last name, pulled an index card from a shoebox, and told me I'd be saving more than $15 on today's purchase. But that wasn't all. I had just earned access to the infamous Carnivore Club! She asked for my e-mail address and said that within a few days I'd start receiving exclusive offers, promotions, and discounts only for Carnivore Club members. (Apparently my total dollars spent over the past few months had reached a certain threshold and so I was given a key to unlock a new and exciting level of perks.) On the way home I detoured to Starbucks, where I held my iPhone out the car window to pay for my Grande Americano. The employee scanned my phone. "Next one's on the house," she said.

Both examples show how two very different companies—one local and low-tech, the other global and high-tech—use loyalty programs to grow their businesses in powerful, highly effective ways. They are classic examples of giving perks to your biggest and most-frequent spenders. However, Joe LaCugna, director of analytics and business intelligence at Starbucks, shared information recently that shook up bloggers, journalists, loyalty experts, and scores of Starbucks fans everywhere when he explained that Starbucks was rewarding its "disloyal" customers more often than its most loyal customers. The better customers—the ones, like myself, who buy a Grande Americano every day—were less likely to receive discounts and promotions from Starbucks than the customers who spend less money and visit the coffee conglomerate less frequently. While most people were busy whining and crying foul that Starbucks could do such a thing to their most loyal customers, I was busy saying to myself, *Here's an organization that actually gets it.* Well, partially. (And I'll explain why only partially shortly.)

Building customer loyalty and advocates for your company doesn't happen overnight, but a loyalty program can help achieve this goal—if (and it is a *big if*) it is done right. Once an organization has fulfilled the basic wants and needs of its customer, it has an opportunity to exceed those wants and needs and develop a deeper relationship to foster increased loyalty. That's why it is important to put systems in place for creating a "ladder of loyal." Any customer can be merely "satisfied," but the next step is moving the customer up the ladder, whereby you are dramatically increasing that customer's satisfaction and delight.

As a customer's loyalty to a company increases, it's up to the company to be aware of that movement and treat the customer accordingly. And, by the way, it doesn't matter if you're B2C or B2B—all the concepts are the same. This chapter isn't just about having the loyalty ladder in place; it's also about implementing systems that allow your customers to willingly and independently ascend that ladder.

In short, on the pages that follow you'll find lots of actionable advice about how to build an effective customer loyalty program—one that will actually work for your organization and generate results. Let's face it. If you're like me, you have a wallet full of cards that don't signify anything even remotely close to genuine customer loyalty. That's because these programs died a long time ago and yet organizations continue to trumpet these halfhearted attempts at loyalty programs as best they can. Is that the best they can do? *Really?* I will show you another way.

WHERE LOYALTY LOST ITS WAY

The rallying cry of failing businesses everywhere is that "There's no such thing as customer loyalty anymore. Loyalty is dead!" But it's not exactly true. Whether they are multinational corporations, Internet start-ups, family-owned businesses, or anything in between, many organizations have learned how to engage their customers and keep them coming back again and again. Let's explore what these organizations are doing differently.

Over the years, a great number of books have seemingly told us everything we could possibly want to know about customer service, customer satisfaction, customer loyalty, and the customer experience. Each year dozens of books are released on these topics. There has been a fair share of more technical books, too, such as Frederick Reichheld's *The Loyalty Effect: The Hidden Force Behind Growth, Profits, and Lasting Value*, which gives larger organizations a fancy measuring device called NPS (net promoter score)—a metric that can be used to gauge customer loyalty. More recently, we've also had books (*New York Times*–bestselling books, no less) that inform businesses that the solution to their woes is simply to start saying "thank you" again, or to do whatever it takes to keep the customer happy, even if it means staying on a customer support call for ten hours! This just isn't a viable solution for every company in this increasingly competitive global marketplace.[1]

I'm more of a pragmatist, and I want my clients to experience dramatic results. Your company may not be able to go into the red just to keep someone happy, and your company might not have the time to wait around until someone tweets or mentions your organization in a digital conversation. There's a better way to tweak and enhance your loyalty-generating efforts—from both a strategic and a tactical level. Let's explore.

The Fallacy of the "Loyalty Program"

Starbucks and my local butcher are the exception. Most loyalty programs are generic and, consequently, fell into the "worthless" pile a long time ago. *Seinfeld* fans will remember how George Costanza's wallet was so stuffed with loyalty cards that it made him sit with a tilt. It's absurd, but it's not far off. We've all opened our wallets or purses to find loads of rewards and points cards that we almost always forget to pull out at the moment of transaction. Or, if you're like me, you have a drawer at home with a stack of these things. It seems as though every business on the planet believes that having a loyalty card is the necessary step to creating customer loyalty.

These cards are not indicative of customer loyalty, of course. And the bigger problem is that most of the cards (and the corresponding programs) don't work as the companies thought they would. Yet every year, organizations continue to waste billions of dollars developing loyalty programs while they fail to build anything even remotely related to customer loyalty. How did we stray so far from our target?

The cards are doing a few things right, though. Points cards are the most common type of loyalty program. We earn points and cash them in for a reward (which might be a freebie, discount, or something else). When we remember to cash in our points, we are thrilled about the stuff we receive. It's always a bonus to receive a free flight or a discount car rental. It might make us feel good for that moment, but what does that mean for customer loyalty? Unfortunately, not much.

Consider this example: The popular (if slightly misleadingly named) Air Miles program in Canada is a syndicated loyalty program where one card can be used to collect points (or miles) at hundreds of different businesses across the country. Those points can then be cashed in for various items such as gift certificates, travel rewards, or household goods. The program is designed to increase customer loyalty. There's no denying it; it's a massively successful rewards program (the parent company—LoyaltyOne Inc.—generates annual revenues of almost $1 billion Canadian).[2]

Almost two-thirds of all Canadian households belong to the Air Miles program. But is it effective? Does it build loyalty toward a specific brand—the type of loyalty we're looking to build with Evergreen relationships? Of course not.

The other problem with points as the ultimate motivator for loyalty is that your customers very quickly determine the value, which can sometimes do more harm than good. One example of where this has happened is Delta Air Lines SkyMiles program. One of the world's largest frequent-flyer communities on the Web, Flyertalk.com, has more than half a million members. The members have renamed Delta's SkyMiles as "Sky Pesos," due to their perceived low value. Each time someone brings up Delta's reward program, some member jumps into the conversation to ensure the correct terminology—*Sky Pesos*—is used. And almost every time, a handful of other members chime in on just how little value the points actually give.

Truth be told, all loyalty programs based on a simple card will influence buying and purchasing behavior, but chances are they won't build anything even remotely close to Evergreen loyalty. Each time I fill up my car, I swipe my Air Miles card, get a few points, and before I know it I have a few thousand points that I can exchange for a gift certificate to Home Depot, or a new watch, or maybe a blender. But I don't believe this is truly meeting the purpose of building "loyalty" to any one particular brand—at least not for me. It certainly hasn't made me feel more partial or more interested in one brand over another. It definitely hasn't made me feel that there's a relationship between myself and any of these companies.

If we can agree that the purpose of increasing loyalty is to give your customers a reason to do business with you and avoid others—mainly your competitors—then we better be darn sure we're developing a relationship that goes beyond the transactional and moves closer to one that's more meaningful and impactful. That takes a lot more than just sticking a swipe card into our customer's (already full) wallets. By the way, we've seen more of these swipe cards moving to mobile devices, which is a step in the right direction, but the main issue, the implementation of the programs, remains a problem.

Let's face it. Loyalty programs have gotten a bad rap, and mostly the critiques are valid. Why? Because, for the most part, they simply don't work. I'm not loyal to any particular airline because of the miles they give me. I'm loyal to first class. I'm not loyal to a specific hotel chain because of my rewards points. Sure, I'm fond of the Mandarin Oriental Hotel Group, but that doesn't mean I'm not willing to stay elsewhere if, say, there isn't a Mandarin Oriental in Providence, Rhode Island (which there's not, by the way … in fact, there aren't many hotel choices at all in Providence). Typically, I'll choose the next best thing or the hotel with the most positive reviews.

So why do we care about building this thing called customer loyalty? Well, for starters loyal customers tend to buy more, and they buy more often, and they're usually cheaper to take care of. They're also more profitable than new customers. So, does it make sense to try to build customer loyalty? Yes. Can a "loyalty program" help you do that? Absolutely! But only if you do it right.

Learning from Starbucks

Do you get a lot of e-mail from Starbucks? You know, a free Grande Latte after 2:00 p.m. or an extra shot of espresso any day this week? Well, congratulations, you're probably one of Starbucks not-so-loyal customers. Why would Starbucks spend more time on someone like you instead of one of its most loyal customers? It's marketing like this that makes most loyalty "experts" scratch their heads. Head scratching commenced when the director of analytics, Joe LaCugna, noted at a Big Data Retail Forum in Chicago in the spring of 2013 that Starbucks had discovered some interesting information about the massive Starbucks loyalty program. Apparently, Starbucks had gathered so much data, from more than 6 million loyalty cardholders, that the company came to an interesting conclusion:

It was better off perking its worst customers and sp[...]
rying about the best customers.[3] When they hear[...]
gers and customer service experts everywhere went a[...].

When you think about it, however, this makes a lot of sense—even though Starbucks shouldn't have needed that much data to gain that insight. Anyway, you see, Starbucks isn't worried about the coffee giant's loyalists; it is most interesting in turning the person who comes to Starbucks every so often into a loyal customer—or at the very least, a more profitable one. The approach is to take low-value customers and turn them into high-value customers. And that's what you should be doing, too.

This is one of the main reasons you should be operating a loyalty program. I work with clients day in and day out, and we carefully look at the data within their loyalty programs to find where their best opportunities exist and how they can further segment their customers to increase customer value. And that, my friend, is one of the keys of a successful customer loyalty program. These programs are designed to reward and perk the best customers for their purchasing habits, sure, but the ultimate goal should be to increase profitability of customers across various segments and the entire organization.

So how is Starbucks doing it? Well, very simply, Starbucks is using its data and segmenting customers according to things like total spend or total visits, and the stores are putting those customers into their own unique marketing programs to increase the frequency of those customers' spending and interaction with the brand. LaCugna and his team believe they don't need to reward the most loyal of their loyal customers since they are already getting perked based on their purchasing habits. (Remember my story about the Grande Americano that I got after I went to the butcher? That was the freebie that I've come to expect after I buy nine of the same.)

While Starbucks is doing so many things right with its loyalty program, this is one area where I think it's wrong and could do better. Here's why: Regardless of how loyal a customer is, there always needs to be a ladder in front of that customer, somewhere for that person to go. When you stick a ladder directly in front of someone, the urge to climb is typically irresistible. Starbucks has an opportunity to use its data to increase the profitability and loyalty of the less loyal customers, sure. But Starbucks also has an opportunity (a huge one, I might add) to take its most loyal customers to an entirely different level of involvement. The problem, though, is that Starbucks is overlooking these customers and, unfortunately, taking us for granted—which is just another variation of our culture's rampant addiction to "new(ish) customers."

And don't think I'm talking about what most experts talk about. They whine that "long-term Starbucks customers are going to be upset; they're not receiving as many deals!" This is not the point. Starbucks is right. The most loyal of the loyal Starbucks customers don't really care about being perked or promoted with coupons or discounts, but there is a better way. After reviewing a few definitions of "customer loyalty," I will show you how.

A Modern Definition of Customer Loyalty

Before we go much further, I think it's important to have a proper understanding of what customer loyalty is, particularly since I believe this term is mostly misunderstood. My trusty iMac dictionary defines loyalty as "the constant support and allegiance to a person or institution." Google the question "What is customer loyalty?" and you'll get different responses, including:

- Customer loyalty is about getting customers to buy, and buy often.

- Customer loyalty is when customers commit themselves and their allegiance to a specific brand.

These definitions come close, but they don't paint the full picture. Here's what I believe the correct definition to be:

Customer loyalty is what happens when an organization
builds and fosters a relationship with a customer based on
consistently positive experiences. Those experiences are capable
of fulfilling needs and wants that are more emotional than
physically tangible, thereby deepening that relationship.
Finally, the relationship provides exceedingly immense value
through the delivery of products, services, or information.

Do you see what I've just defined? The Three Cs framework. To foster and nurture customer loyalty we need to stop considering various aspects of our organizations—such as customer acquisition and customer retention—as independent functions, and understand that customer loyalty is something that culminates naturally when the Three Cs are employed in a thoughtful manner to create a cohesive customer experience. Furthermore, customer loyalty happens before, during, and after the actual sale. When viewed in this manner, it becomes clear that the purpose of loyalty programs is to help us gain a better understanding of our customers and tailor specific marketing messages toward different subsets of customers.

For many companies, customer loyalty can seem like a pie-in-the-sky ideal. "Sure, it's a good idea," they say. "But does it really exist? Are customers *genuinely* interested in having a long-term relationship with the companies they do business with?" The answer is a resounding yes! I've helped restaurants, hotels, plumbers, golf clubs, and auto mechanics build real, emotionally driven customer loyalty. To do that, though, you need to embrace the Three Cs framework and go beyond—far, far beyond—the simple points card.

DEVELOPING (OR REFINING) YOUR LOYALTY PROGRAM

Now that we can all agree that loyalty programs—at least the way they used to be designed—are gone, and gone forever, it's time for you to develop a new type of loyalty program. Throughout the rest of this chapter, I'll explain how to structure a rewards program that actually works, and how to think about your best customers, both strategically and tactically. The first thing to realize is this: Creating a loyalty program is more about process than perfection. Communities are built by having a number of different structures in place. Customer loyalty programs aren't much different. By building effective systems for capturing and rewarding customer loyalty, your business will benefit from the ability to:

- Enhance your customer experience for your most valuable customers.

- Retain customers longer.

- Maximize value of your best and most loyal customers.

This list could go on and on. The benefits derived from a properly defined loyalty program are endless. Let's see how it's done.

Understanding the Objectives of an Effective Loyalty Program

A properly functioning loyalty program will increase the profitability of an organization. Starbucks needed the data of more than 6 million loyal members to tell them money could be made with customers who shopped with them less frequently. *Duh!* You don't need even a fraction of that data to come to a similar conclusion. What you do need is a proper understanding of what makes a loyalty program effective. Three distinct objectives need to drive the overarching strategy of any loyalty program:

1. To increase customer retention and increase the frequency of purchases and also the size of each transaction

2. To gain a better understanding of your customers, including actionable insights

3. To generate authentic, segmented, and individualized communication and messaging

All three sound pretty good, don't they? Obviously increasing the frequency of purchases and the size of each transaction is pretty exciting. Of course, knowing more about your customers and what they like could also be pretty valuable. Imagine how your marketing return on investment (ROI) would change if you were able to generate highly targeted and specific marketing messages. It sure is more exciting to be at the top of a tree and looking down, rather than the other way around. Are you gaining altitude yet?

Identifying How the Program Fits Within Your Big Picture

How does your organization create an effective loyalty program—one that goes beyond punch cards and point accumulations? The thing to remember is that you need to keep your current customers cradled in your loving arms as much as humanly possible. Let's face it. We're all navigating choppy waters when it comes to customer acquisition. It's more expensive than ever before, and that's one of the major reasons we are finally seeing organizations turn the tide to focus on what matters most—retaining their current customers. A customer loyalty program isn't the only factor in the equation when it comes to increasing customer loyalty; it's simply a small dab of glue in the big scheme of things. Organizations are under immense pressure to bring current customers back more often, and that's really what this book is about. But the solution comes from an organizationwide shift and understanding that business has changed; things aren't the way they used to be.

A report from a top-tier loyalty association claimed that "marketing is now playing a role in the loyalty equation." *Gee... Do you think?* I'm shocked and saddened to read such things. When did marketing ever *not* play a role in the loyalty equation? I hope this far into the book you've realized that every facet of your business is "playing a role" in the loyalty equation—especially marketing. I find it hard to believe that this observation comes as a revelation to some people.

Your goal in building your corporate character in a way that identifies with your ideal customer archetype is to ensure your success when it comes to retention and loyalty. Don't worry, I won't tell you that it costs ten times more to acquire a new customer than it does to keep (or sell to) an existing one. If you've read this far, you already know that. Customer loyalty is the result of consistent, day-to-day marketing.

Building Your Loyalty Ladder

When thinking about creating a loyalty program, you need to consider your ascension ladder. Unfortunately, most organizations don't. Here's what typically happens: A medium-size restaurant decides to start a loyalty card program. For every dollar spent, the customer will earn a point. And for every 400 points, the customer will earn a predetermined reward. That's the loyalty program. That's it. All done. Call it a day!

The problem is that the company has built a "ladder" that consists of one single step, and there is nowhere for customers to go after they take that first step. This is the biggest mistake companies make. The next biggest mistake is that companies think customers will actually take that first step. Most won't. If you go this route with your loyalty program, both you and your customers will be disappointed. (And, really, shame on you for wasting such a wonderful opportunity!) Don't fret, though, if this sounds like your company, because you can still turn the tide. I'm here to help.

But first, let's review another typical problem with rewards cards, as illustrated with this example. I went to buy a frozen yogurt at a new shop in my local mall. While I was checking out, the young woman asked me if I wanted join the store's exclusive loyalty program. I asked two questions:

- What makes it exclusive?

- What can I expect?

"Well, it's not really exclusive," she replied, "but you'll get a lot of great promotions and coupons." No loyalty ladder, and certainly no purpose. This is backward and the epitome of a poorly designed loyalty program. If it's so exclusive, then why can anyone join? Not to mention, the timing of the request was off: I hadn't even tasted the product yet.

You need a ladder. There should be multiple rungs that a customer can continue to climb.

Most important, as the customer climbs the ladder, so does his or her emotional commitment to you and your brand. Likewise, your involvement in the relationship with the customer should also increase. It's your duty to create a ladder of loyalty that your customers can climb. Here's the thing about ladders: We all know they are designed to be climbed. That's their purpose. And that's what we've all been conditioned to do (except for the dolt who walks *under* the ladder). If we don't present a ladder to our customers, then we're not giving them anywhere to go.

Consider for a moment the following visual. Imagine you are looking at a high-rise building that's transparent and entirely built of windows. On each floor you can see people hanging out and doing things. Each floor is like a party. And the party gets better the higher you go. You've got to show your customers what's happening on the fifteenth floor and why they should want to climb the ladder to the penthouse.

Prioritizing Status over Stuff

In all probability, everything people in your organization thought they knew about customer loyalty is wrong. Particularly if they thought loyalty was earned through size and frequency of purchase. Particularly if they believed they could essentially buy more loyalty through points and rewards. The problem is that customers care far less about rewards and "stuff" than they do about recognition, appreciation, and value.

In his classic book, *Drive: The Surprising Truth About What Motivates Us*, thought leader Daniel Pink inadvertently shows us why most loyalty programs don't work as well as they could when he examines employees and what motivates them to do their best work. Pink explains that historically most organizations have motivated employees though extrinsic rewards (think: cash bonuses), but that is a thing of the past. Today's organizations must recognize that what really drives people professionally are intrinsic motivators such as autonomy, mastery, and purpose.[4]

Pink's work can transform the way we think about customer loyalty programs. Don't get me wrong, customers like perks and rewards, but customers in today's digitally interconnected society want more. Just as connection and community can trump what it is you actually offer to customers (your content), intrinsic rewards can trump the tangible rewards we've traditionally used to increase loyalty. Loyalty programs have typically been built on extrinsic motivators (external rewards, such as cash back, points, discounts, and more stuff) as opposed to intrinsic motivators (internal rewards such as status and recognition). Your loyalty program should be focused on the intrinsic and tied into all your community structures. In a nutshell, your customers are far less concerned about earning stuff than they are about the recognition that comes from various levels of loyalty. Customers want to feel appreciated and recognized. How can you better recognize your customers?

A client of mine has an information-based website. It's a subscription model where customers pay a monthly fee for access. Given the high price point, he only gets about a dozen new customers each month. (That's actually all he needs.) Each month he does a free webinar for all existing and new customers. What he does next is interesting. During each monthly webinar he introduces all new members by showing their names and congratulating them on joining the exclusive club. He takes a moment to thank each one of them individually. In so doing, he simultaneously recognizes the new customers and creates camaraderie among existing members of the community. He doesn't have to give away points; this small token of appreciation and recognition is powerful enough. Often the smallest stuff has the biggest impact. Now I know personalized introductions aren't feasible if your company gets dozens, hundreds, or thousands of new customers each month, but think about it: What *is* possible?

Showing Customers What They Can't Have

People want what other people can't have. It's human nature. And this tendency can be used as a powerful incentive. One of my small-business clients who runs a restaurant decided to show people exactly what they couldn't have. Each month, he attaches a supplementary dining menu to the normal menu. The difference is that *only* loyalty members can order these items. No exceptions. "Not even the Pope can order from this menu without a card!" one menu read. He is very serious. If you aren't a member, you simply cannot have these items. Servers learned to handle customer requests in a fun way, suggesting they consider joining the loyalty program. Some customers aren't pleased, but I think it's brilliant. The restaurant signs up hundreds of new members each time it runs such a promotion.

Another interesting component of this specific loyalty program is that my client charges a $20 fee to join. This charge accomplishes a few things. Most important, it distinguishes between those who are serious about joining and those who will have another useless card in their wallet. It also creates an incentive for the customer to take care of the card. ("After all, I paid for this card; I better keep it, and use it.") New members are given a "welcome package" when they join the program, which contains a $20 gift certificate that can be used on a future visit. Interestingly, my client has noted that the average spend on that second visit is typically almost 70 percent higher than the original purchase. Brilliant! Could your company do something similar?

What could you offer that others can't have? I've worked with hundreds of people who own and operate membership-based businesses. Most of them are online, but I've helped a number of off-line companies successfully implement the concept of membership in their businesses. People thrive on being part of a group of "belongers," or those who have access to something others don't, or can't, have. The true power of the membership, though, comes from packaging your products, services, or offerings and committing your customers to buying regularly and frequently—on autopilot. It's a win for them, and a major win for you. Almost any business can find a unique way to offer some sort of membership—from the barber, to the car wash, to the driving range, to the restaurant. How could your business?

Selling Loyalty

You can't buy loyalty, but you can sell it. A moment ago you read about my client who charges $20 to join his loyalty program. It's a smart move to have customers offset the cost of the program. Aside from the obvious practical benefits that it offers the company, this approach also increases the chances that a customer will actually use the service and become loyal. So why not consider a loyalty program that customers pay for, and then earn perks associated with membership?

Consider one of the more famous programs, Amazon Prime. For $99 a year customers can join Amazon Prime and receive a whole slew of benefits. For example, Prime members receive free two-day shipping on anything Amazon sells, all the time, with no minimum order. Prime members can borrow books from the Kindle Owners' Lending Library for free. (Remember Jeff Bezos's "Dear Muggles" letter, recounted in Chapter 3, when he announced that the entire Harry Potter series was available for Kindle owners?) Most recently, Amazon has decided to go head-to-head with the popular Netflix service, and Prime members are now able to stream books and movies from an instant library of more than 40,000 items.

I've been a Prime member for three years, and it's worth every penny. I can't tell you how often I have needed something and have had it delivered within two days. (Prime members can also have any Prime-eligible item sent overnight for only $3.99.) It's a great program, and Amazon has certainly experienced an increase in the frequency of transactions from me since I joined.

What's the difference between Amazon's program and one that could be run by someone who owns a small company? Not much. In fact, that same restaurant client mentioned previously introduced a Mug Club for craft beer aficionados. By segmenting his customers and identifying the ones who simply loved to try new beers, he launched a VIP club with a $79 fee. Members receive their own mug on display at the restaurant, a bronze plaque with their name, an extra four-ounce pour with every beer, on every visit, and a whole pile of other added benefits. He sold 100 memberships within a matter of days and soon ran out of spots for mugs. In addition, the "club" now actually feels like a club. Nobody wants to lose their spot, and many patrons have renewed for a second year.

The Mug Club now has a waiting list, and my client constantly receives e-mails from friends of members begging for just "one more mug." People love to see their name in bright lights. It makes them feel important and recognized. In this case, each customer enjoys seeing his or her name on the bar accompanied by a coveted mug spot. It makes each customer think: *I'm a star!*

Make *your* customers the stars of the show. The motivation that comes from being recognized is far more valuable than the actual product or service being delivered. I'll ask again: Why couldn't you apply these ideas to your business? Whether you operate a B2C or B2B company, the ideas work the same way. It might require a little thought and creativity, but it certainly is possible to do in any industry, for any product.

The membership model is all around. Don't for a minute think your business couldn't create some sort of membership offering, because I'm sure you can come up with something. Consider airline lounges. Are these any different from other VIP clubs? Nope.

In addition to the membership model, consider creating an offering that allows your customers the chance to either earn or buy their way into a program that offers unique access. Here's another example. If you have kids and you have money, you can go to Disney and skip the lines using Disney's VIP Tour Services. For $340 per hour, you can skip the lines at the attractions, travel in a private vehicle, and gain VIP seating to shows. I realize this is less of a loyalty program and more of a VIP program that can be purchased. But could you apply the same concept to your own business? Of course you could! What could your customers buy access to that increases convenience or speed of delivery, or access to your content? What could customers buy access to that increases the frequency of purchase with your company?

Could a restaurant allow you to skip the line or have priority access to reservation slots? Imagine if a restaurant proactively called its most loyal customers on Monday to secure their reservations for Friday night (or, more important, let's say it reached out to the most loyal customers who hadn't visited in a while). Talk about standing out from the crowd! Airlines let the customers with the most points on their loyalty program snag any open first-class seats. Why couldn't you create similar levels of VIP access within your organization? You can, and you should.

DESIGNING YOUR CUSTOMER
LOYALTY ACTION PLAN

Customers can be fascinating. There's no doubt about it. But your customers aren't going to keep the conversation going. A loyalty program can help, but it should be just one aspect of your broader attempts to build meaningful and long-lasting relationships with your customers. A loyalty program is also not the be-all and end-all to increased profits and organizational growth, but it can offer a tremendous opportunity to gain knowledge and understanding of your customer base, and increase the profitability of your current customers. If we are being really honest, customer loyalty is created through consistent and regular marketing and actions, not just a single program.

Nevertheless, with a properly structured loyalty plan in place, your existing customers will continually move up the rungs of a carefully designed ladder of loyalty. This, in turn, should allow you to increase the revenues from your best customers, and increase loyalty and revenue from your less-profitable customers. Don't waste this opportunity by providing cheap points and lousy rewards. Consider this a golden opportunity to learn more about your customers and what makes them tick. An effective loyalty program combines customer data and behaviors so that you can offer a more personalized and specific experience for that customer or specific segment of customers. Remember your different archetypes? You can (and should) create specific levels of loyalty for each group.

You can't buy customer loyalty, but if you are not paying attention to it, you're missing a massive opportunity to increase customer retention, referrals, and customer value. The key to an effective loyalty program is that it allows you to identify your most valuable customers and (as we saw in the Starbucks example) your lower-value customers, and to design programs and initiatives to create the type of behaviors you want from both groups. Let me provide a commonsense approach to properly structuring your loyalty program for maximum effectiveness. I've helped organizations design loyalty programs that allow them to identify both their best customers and (more important) those who offer opportunity for massive growth. Figure 7-1 shows what the traditional model of customer loyalty looks like.

FIGURE 7-1

Traditional Loyalty Programs

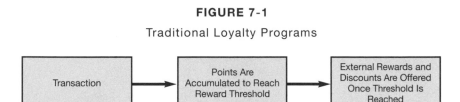

Now, contrast that model to what's happening when you structure your ladder of loyalty the right way, as shown in Figure 7-2.

FIGURE 7-2

The Evergreen Ladder of Loyalty

THE PENTHOUSE SUITE
Your Highest Level
of Intimacy
Show all customers the
upper levels, experiences,
and benefits derived by your
best and most loyal
customers.

When customers reach
the top, the external
rewards should be more
valuable, less frequent,
and more surprising.

Intrinsic rewards continue

INCREASED SUPPORT
When a customer reaches
this level, responsiveness
should increase.

Intrinsic rewards continue
External rewards continue

INCREASED INTIMACY
What can certain
customers have/do/access
that others can't?

Intrinsic rewards continue
External rewards continue

Give customers the
ability to summit to
the top quickly.

• Offer paid subscriptions.

• Recognize high-volume
purchases.

• Recognize increased
frequency early.

EXTERNAL REWARDS
Use external rewards to
encourage usage and
consumption and
participation.

Always be mindful of
good behaviors!
Recognize and reward
customer referrals, or
customers who go
above and beyond the
call of duty!

External rewards continue

RECOGNIZE AND
REWARD INTRINSIC
MOTIVATIONS
Recognize and reward
behaviors like
consumption and
participation
in your community.

External rewards begin...

NEW CUSTOMERS
Effective marketing
attracts the right
customer archetypes.
Always be showing
customers what happens
as their loyalty to your
company increases.

Don't you want to learn how to build an Evergreen Ladder of Loyalty? It really is not all that hard. You just need to follow the six simple steps detailed below.

Step One: Define Your Objectives

Everything your business does needs to be carefully designed to meet specific objectives. Your loyalty program is no different. As we've discussed, too often loyalty programs aren't given the type of attention they deserve. Sure, it's easy to just give people a card and start rewarding them with points, but this is not very effective, and it won't provide the type of results you're looking for. It also won't help you create the type of relationships that are long term and Evergreen. Articulate your objectives for your loyalty program. They might include:

- Increasing customer value and profitability of various customer segments

- Growing the size of the customer database

- Increasing the transaction size and frequency of customer spending

- Developing more targeted marketing based on insights gained about customers

- Retaining customers longer

- Acquiring more new customers

- Building long-lasting customer relationships

- Reducing advertising and marketing costs

- Increasing word-of-mouth and recommendations among customers

I would recommend all of the above objectives as a wonderful starting point. Again, though, I provide this list purely as a starting point for you and your team (if you have one). This list will need to be customized for your company. It is necessary to develop clear-cut objectives. When the objectives for what you plan to do with the customer data and the increased insights you're bound to gain *aren't* carefully defined ahead of time, you run the risk of running your loyalty program in the least effective way possible. This means your loyalty program database is likely to become another list of customers who all receive the same marketing, promotions, and discounts.

Another reason why it is so important to consider the objectives from the get-go is that it's hard to make significant changes once you've kicked off a loyalty program. Once you've loaded your customers with cards or key tags, or have started doling out points to reward purchasing behavior, it's both difficult and expensive to end the program if it's not working the way you expected. In addition, you can expect your customers to have negative reactions if you change the rules mid-game.

The point of determining your objectives is to very carefully consider the outcomes you want to achieve from your program. You may not know exactly the type of outcome you'd like to achieve, and that's okay. Your program should be fluid enough to morph and grow; that's fine. But you want to ensure you are oriented in the right direction.

Step Two: Determine What You Want to Learn

Forget "big data." Focus on small data, and the types of insights that will help you grow your company. After you determine your overall objectives and how they fit into your company's organizational framework, decide what you want to happen as a result of your loyalty program. This is really about determining the type of data you'll use your loyalty program to capture. I would suggest the following data to start:

- Demographic data

- Purchase frequency

- Transaction size

- Recency of last purchase

You'll also want to articulate how you define an extremely loyal customer to your business. Is your definition based on a certain threshold of spending? If so, what's that number? You need to give careful thought to the data you need to capture. Sometimes more can be better. You never want to build a program only to realize—thousands or even millions of members later—that you didn't capture a vital piece of information.

Step Three: Design Your Loyalty Program

Certain basics should be a part of every loyalty program. For instance, every loyalty program must give customers the things they want. As we've already discussed, more often than not your customers want the intrinsic benefits that come from recognition more than they want rewards. With that said, rewards are a key component. For a loyalty program to be truly effective, it must maintain a balance between rewards, offers, and communication with customers based on their individual attitudes, purchasing behaviors, demographics, and psychographics. Therefore, you need to define your benefit structure for your customers carefully. Here are some questions to get you thinking about how to structure your program:

- *Is it a points-based program?* If so, how is the customer rewarded? Do the points turn into a cash discount, or are customers able to redeem points for multiple perks?

- *Do cardholders/members experience additional perks?* For instance, do they receive an immediate discount at the time of purchase? Do they receive free shipping? Do they receive extended customer support?

- *Do you have any surprise gifts or bonuses that customers receive once they spend a certain amount?* (Hint: You should.)

- *How often will you make exclusive offers to loyalty members?*

- *Will you reward certain behaviors, or just purchases?* (Hint: If you are building community structures, which I hope by now you've realized you must, then I strongly urge you to reward the type of loyal behaviors you would like to reinforce.) As we discussed a few pages back, simply because someone carries your card, and even makes frequent purchases from your company, doesn't necessarily mean the person is a loyal customer.

- *Do different customer archetypes require different rewards?* And if so, what are they? You need to remember your various customer archetypes and should create rewards specific to them. Perhaps you let them choose. It doesn't really matter. What does matter is that you build rewards and recognition levels for each different group.

There's nothing wrong with adjusting your program's structure later, but for now, it's crucial to carefully consider and map out (to the best of your current ability) how you'll design your loyalty program.

Step Four: Identify Metrics of Success

You will have costs associated with creating the loyalty program, maintaining it, and distributing your incentives. Every loyalty initiative includes various costs. Time and energy (major investments, in and of themselves) are also required to do it right. With all of this output, you need to know that the program is going to be worth the investment. I don't blame you. You need to determine what key metrics you will use to gauge the success of your program. These are your indicators of success and progress. It's important that you are clear on your measures or indicators so that at any given time you can review the ROI and adjust your program as required. Don't forget behavioral measures, such as increased engagement or participation. You can't judge loyalty primarily on direct financial impact.

Loyalty program metrics might be identified by answering these questions:

- Is the value of your customer base increasing?

- Is the value of an individual member/customer increasing? (For example, is the customer spending more now than before becoming a member? Is the person shopping with your business more frequently?)

- Has your customer attrition decreased?

- Are loyalty members generally happier and more pleased with your product or service?

- Do loyalty members contribute more to the community? Are they more engaged?

You want to be sure you are actively measuring and monitoring your efforts so that you can tweak or adjust later, if necessary.

Step Five: Construct Your Program

Aside from building the ins and outs of how you'll recognize and reward your customers, you need to think about how you'll structure your program. For example, questions might include:

- How and when will you enroll customers?

- Will there be a fee to join?

- What will new members receive?

- Will you have ongoing communications and/or promotions?

- Is everyone automatically a member?

Sometimes everyone who makes a single purchase automatically becomes a member of a particular club. Here's an example: I bought a new Audi. A month later, I received my first copy of the car's official magazine. It was chock-full of value—this is what you call great *content* supported by *character* and *community*! It took me well beyond the transaction of simply buying a new car. I read the magazine from cover to cover.

A few months later I received another package in the mail. I opened it to find a beautiful, full-color folder with a black VIP card and a personalized letter from the company. The letter asked me how I was enjoying my vehicle and if there was anything the automaker could do for me. The materials told me all about the benefits of the black VIP card and how I could use it for complimentary roadside assistance and a number of other perks. In this case, I was automatically enrolled into the "VIP" program. The program was carefully designed to gain further emotional attachment from me to both Audi's character and community. This is an example of a well-constructed loyalty program. Does it give you any ideas for how you might construct yours? I hope so.

Step Six: Surprise Your Customers Constantly

The problem with building a loyalty program that's structured based on rewards, or even levels of loyalty, is that it gets stale rather quickly. Most of these programs do. As big a fan that I am of the Starbucks loyalty program, it's gotten somewhat boring. I already know what gold level gets me. There's no surprise. It's the same old, year after year.

From time to time you need to refresh your loyalty program and the benefits associated with it for your customers. Of course, if a customer expects to receive a certain reward that you've stipulated, then it's not worth changing that reward at the expense of upsetting the customer.

I'm simply talking about *adding* unexpected perks from time to time. Customers should constantly be surprised. Imagine the delight if your top-tier customers (say, your top 20 percent) received Christmas cards with a handwritten letter and small gift card as a token of your appreciation. However, this idea might not work in New York City (or any other metropolitan hub that embraces a religiously diverse population). In this case, imagine if your CEO (who might just be you!) personally called ten of your best-spending clients? Would they be surprised? Or what if you invited twenty of your highest-spending customers to a lavish breakfast event at the Trump SoHo New York? No matter where you do business, don't you think any one of these ideas would be a better investment of your marketing dollars than simply blasting your entire customer base with some generic promotional message?

However you choose to enhance your loyalty program, just remember what I'm going to call "the Starbucks Rule." (I'm using this term somewhat tongue in cheek, since Starbucks didn't follow this rule.) Never discredit your top-tier and most loyal customers or, heaven forbid, take them for granted. Far from it. Use your loyalty program as a profit-generating tool to increase the value of your less frequent and less valuable customers, sure. But also use it to increase involvement from and connection with your evangelists.

Thankfully, you didn't need 6 million members to give you that insight. I'm glad I could be of service!

CHAPTER 8

Articulating a New Approach to Customer Service

Tending to Your Garden (and Pulling Those Weeds!)

In 2004, real estate mogul Donald Trump tried to trademark the phrase "You're fired!" His request was made in the light of his hit reality television series, *The Apprentice.* Thinking back to the first C of an Evergreen organization—character—Trump is a prime example of someone who's become a *character* larger than himself. He has taken the persona of The Donald to such extremes that one could argue he's even become a caricature of himself—a classic example of the concept of "the Facebook You," as discussed in Chapter 3.

Trump has been mocked and laughed at. He's hosted *Saturday Night Live* twice and has been impersonated by the cast more than twenty-four times since 2004. Trump has filed for bankruptcy at least four times,[1] and he has engaged in widely publicized feuds with other celebrities, including a long-standing media battle with Rosie O'Donnell. He has promoted himself in the world of professional (aka *fake*) wrestling, including a match called the "Battle of Billionaires" at WrestleMania 23, where the loser agreed to shave his head. No matter what happens, Trump is relentless in his shameless self-promotion. Trump's request to trademark "You're fired!" was denied, by the way.

So what does this story have to do with Evergreen marketing, you might ask? Well, it's one thing to fire an employee, but can you fire a customer? And why in the world would you want to—especially after you've worked so hard to get that customer in the first place? I'll tell you why: The reality is that the customer is *not* always right.

That may come as a surprise to you—especially since another message has flooded the airwaves in recent years. No doubt you've heard a tremendous amount about Zappos, the mega online shoe retailer whose story I relayed in Chapter 3. But there's more to the tale. Zappos, the brainchild of CEO Tony Hsieh, took the idea of "*wow* customer service" to an entirely new level. Essentially, Zappos said to its employees something along the lines of: "Let's do whatever it takes to make keeping customers fun." And that they did! Dozens of stories about Zappos have been featured in the media: From ten-hour customer service calls, to customer service reps ordering pizzas for customers, to Zappos taking back hundreds of pairs of shoes from a family whose mother had passed away. The last time I checked, there were forty-four books on Amazon with "Zappos" in the title, and more than 5,000 additional customer service–related books that either referenced Zappos or were almost exclusively devoted to analyzing the success of the company.

With nearly every other marketing and customer service expert jumping on the let's-write-a-book-about-Zappos-as-a-model-of-customer-service bandwagon, the dialogue has become highly skewed. In truth, the Zappos way *isn't* the only way—and there's a good chance it's not *your* way. In fact, even Hsieh himself was willing to divulge a dirty little secret about business in his book *Delivering Happiness: A Path to*

Profits, Passion, and Purpose: Not every customer is worth keeping. Hsieh wrote: "Realize that it's okay to fire customers who are insatiable or abuse your employees."[2]

In this chapter I'll breach topics most organizations are afraid to discuss, such as which customers you should fire. The simple fact is that often organizations spend time, money, and resources keeping customers and meeting unreasonable demands from customers who should be cut loose. Just like we have to prune limbs from trees to keep them healthy and let them grow stronger, companies often need to cut customers for similar reasons. I'll present methods for you (or your team, if you have one) to use when dealing with the demands of an irate customer; a model for determining the validity of complaints, criticisms, and feedback; and how to know which customers aren't worth keeping. This is a far more tactical chapter than those that preceded it, getting into the nitty-gritty details about customer service and other customer-related issues.

Let's press onward.

GIVING YOURSELF PERMISSION
TO FIRE BAD CUSTOMERS

In Chapter 1, I observed at the outset that it is a profoundly revolutionary time to be operating a business. Our customers are more knowledgeable than ever before. They have the upper hand in their ability to exert, expect, and demand the way they'll do business and with whom. To survive, organizations must think about customers and their experiences in an entirely new way. Then I asked, "So what's next?"

There's a problem with my question, though. Did you catch it? I made the same critical error that almost everyone else is making. But I caught myself. We all know customers have changed. This isn't exactly breaking news. We all know we are living in a newly connected world where our customers are talking to people they don't know, and to each other. We all know that customers can jump on social media the first time our companies make a mistake. We all know some customers believe that they've hit us good with negative reviews on Yelp, or brash phone calls to our customer service teams because we might have shipped the wrong product or taken a little too long to deliver it.

The mistake I made, though, back in Chapter 1, is that not only did I ask the wrong question, but I also answered it. Do you remember how I answered the "What's next" question? I said that we all need to become even more customer-centric. I could have left things at that—but that would make me no different than the 5,000 experts who decided to feature Zappos in their books.

Now is the time to be more nuanced in articulating what I mean by being customer-centric. I believe we need to be clear on who our best customers are, but we also need to be clear on the type of customer we *don't* want. Furthermore, we need to have the courage to fire those customers. Here's why: Remember again how, in Chapter 1, we discussed the true value of our customers? I made reference to the Pareto principle, also known as the 80/20 rule. In brief, almost 80 percent of all results tend to come from 20 percent of the action. In other words, your data teams can show you who the top 20 percent of your customers are. These customers are likely responsible for 80 percent of your profits. *These* are the customers you want to dedicate time, energy, and resources to when it comes to customer service.

But view your company's statistics from another angle and you'll find that the Pareto principle still holds up. Your data teams should be able to identify the 20 percent of your customers who are creating 80 percent of your problems. Now *these* are the customers you want to fire—and it's okay to do so. In fact, it is not only okay, but you owe it to your good and loyal customers to do precisely that!

Now that you've given yourself permission to fire your bad customers, it is time to name names. Let's start culling the herd.

DETERMINING WHICH CUSTOMERS YOU SHOULD (AND SHOULDN'T) FIRE

When it comes to firing customers, I have a few simple rules of my own. Customers who are rude, racist, sexist, or vulgar should be free to pack their bags *immediately*. Give this customer the pink slip. Don't worry about profitability in these situations; worry about employee morale. That being said, if the customer service dynamic gets heated and any of our employees lose their cool, we must also take a stand against rude, racist, sexist, or vulgar comments made to our customers. This is, after all, a two-way street.

When it comes to customer service, people can get downright nasty. Historically, the telephone has allowed people to show their nasty side, since they do not have to look anyone in the eye. The Internet, however, takes this dynamic to a whole new level. There has been a dramatic rise in keyboard cowboys and Internet trolls in recent years. These are the folks who come out with guns ablaze when things go awry. We've all been on sites with reviews of products and services, and sometimes it's hard to believe the things people will write. Let them go. These customers aren't worth your time or even your response. I believe this wholeheartedly, even if the mistake was originally yours.

Now that we've reviewed the undesirable customers who will inevitably surface, let's review the other customers who you need to do a bit of research to identify. You'll face two types of bad customers on the chopping block: problem children and Hungry Hippos. It may sound unpleasant, but allow me to introduce you to each in turn.

Your Problem Children

The problem child is the customer who is insatiable and never content—regardless of how well you do. This person is, quite simply, never happy, for whatever reason. Some people are just like this. We all know problem children. They're constantly whining that people are taking advantage of them. Either that, or they're complaining about one thing or another. In essence, they either can't be pleased or they make it almost impossible for us to feel as if they are pleased.

In most businesses these customers are the easiest to identify. They are typically the lowest-value, most price-sensitive customers you have. There's very little chance these customers will ever exhibit the qualities of genuinely loyal customers. They're not going to be enamored with the emotionally engaging experience you are creating for your customers. In fact, quite the contrary: Problem children often grow up and become Hungry Hippos.

Your Hungry Hippos

In the classic Hasbro board game Hungry Hungry Hippos, players whack a lever that causes their hippo to "eat" a marble. The player whose hippo eats the most marbles wins. Every business is full of Hungry Hippos, and we are partially to blame. After all, we keep feeding them marbles. It's surprising to many of us to learn that even profitable customers aren't always worth keeping—not if they're Hungry Hippos. While these customers may be considered "loyal" from a repeat visit/purchase standpoint, they are also intent on sucking you dry to ensure they get their money's worth.

Some customers cost considerably more to serve than others, even customers who spend more. You see, even though some people may be "great spenders," this doesn't necessarily make them "high value" customers, especially if we don't have a clear picture of what those customers actually cost. Some customers make excessive service requests, or abuse product consumption and usage limits. This means that, when it comes to growing your organization, it's sometimes more beneficial to focus on your less profitable customers.

Consider the following examples: the retail customer who buys an outfit, wears it, and then returns it (it happens!); the e-book purchaser who reads the book within a day or two and then requests a refund; the restaurant patron who takes "unlimited refills or endless pasta" to an almost obscene level. Each and every day, organizations pander to the Hungry Hippos. The problem is that Hungry Hippos attempt to take advantage of what you do—and you serve them at a great expense to your organization. Let's look at another example of Hungry Hippos and how they often attempt to "overeat" their share, even with larger organizations.

In a famous example, in 2007 Sprint canceled the accounts of more than 1,000 customers. At first, this decision seemed like a travesty. How could a company do such a thing? How could a company fire paying customers just for calling customer support? We learned later on that these customers were actually Hungry Hippos. They were calling Sprint repeatedly, claiming that they were receiving bad service and scamming the company for credits or discounts off their bills. Sprint argued that these customers were literally defrauding the company.[3] And they probably were.

Hungry Hippos will continue to take advantage of loopholes and find any opportunity to take more and give less. It's no secret that some people act this way. Some iPhone apps provide direct phone numbers and word-for-word scripts that people can use to call their cable, cell phone, and utility companies and negotiate deals on their contracts. Of course, there is "wiggle room" in many of these contracts. Most of us have experienced this inadvertently when we have canceled a service, such as cable, only to be called by the company later and offered a significant discount to return. In this case, you may have found yourself thinking, *If I can pay $29.95 a month now, why was I paying $89.95 for the past seven years?* Alas, the wiggle room itself is beyond the scope of our present discussion. The point here is that some people go out of their way to take advantage of company policies.

Amazon, a company that I described earlier as one of the most customer-centric businesses on the planet, is also using data to fire its Hungry Hippos. One user on the message board Blu-ray.com shared the following experience and an e-mail received from Amazon,[4] stating that the customer's account was closed due to excessive negative complaints and returns:

Hello,

A careful review of your account indicates that you've requested replacements or refunds on a majority of your orders for a variety of reasons.

In the normal course of business, we expect there may be occasional problems. However, the rate at which such problems have occurred on your account is extraordinary, and it cannot continue. Effective immediately, your Amazon.com account is closed, and you will no longer be able to shop in our store.

All other accounts related to yours have also been closed. If you were to open a new account, it would also be closed. We will not accept the return of any additional orders placed under a new account, and we won't issue further refunds for those orders. We appreciate your cooperation.

Going forward, any questions must be directed to cis@amazon.com. Please do not contact Amazon's Customer Service department, as they will no longer be able to assist you.

Best regards,
Account Specialist
Amazon.com

The user in question claimed this wasn't the case, just as Sprint's customers claimed they weren't defrauding the company. Of course, we'll never know the full stories. Nor do we need to. The simple fact is that sometimes it makes *good business sense* to fire a customer. If you are a business owner, I want you to realize that there is a lot of talk about how customers now have control, but if you want to grow and thrive, then *you* need to maintain control. Amazon and Sprint are dealing with their Hungry Hippos, and you should be, too.

Shortly, I'll show you exactly how to handle these situations as eloquently as possible. But first, I want to make sure that you are clear, very clear, on a category of customers that you want to make sure to keep.

Your Least Profitable Customers

Now that we've determined that some customers need to be fired—and fired *immediately*—it's time to switch gears. You see, over the past few years some experts have suggested that businesses have two types of customers—high value and low value—and that our focus needs to be only on the former. These same people have been saying that we need to fire our least profitable customers. I disagree with this approach—strongly!

If you start from a position where you recognize that every customer who enters your business has massive potential value, then you can't simply make a decision to fire customers who are currently low value. Instead, you need to cultivate them. As we saw with Starbucks in the last chapter, low-value customers can—with the right marketing—be turned into high-value customers.

Remember in Chapter 1 we discussed how some organizations are willing to gamble with their most valuable asset? In fact, many organizations make this critical error in judgment. Your base of customers determines the current value of your business. Furthermore, this asset (your current customers) is the primary source of your company's expected future value (gauged by both the anticipated profits from current customers as well as any new business/referrals that they generate). Businesses should consider the value of an existing customer based on that customer's potential future value. Likewise, businesses will only know which customers to focus marketing efforts on (and how) if they segment the data that they collect and move forward in a thoughtful and strategic manner.

Be careful not to fall into the trap of firing customers simply based on their perceived (current, low) value. Go ahead and fire your Hungry Hippos and problem children. They're not worth your time, energy, and expense. But your less profitable customers? *They* are almost always worth your efforts.

A COMMONSENSE APPROACH
TO CUSTOMER SERVICE

We've all experienced the type of customer service that makes us want to pull our hair out. Do you remember the last time you were treated poorly when you interacted with a business? You may have been told that your call was extremely important, and then gone on to wait for thirty-five minutes. You may have been treated rudely in a store. We've all had experiences like these, even with companies that claim to be focused on the customer. The company claims to care about us, but it sure doesn't feel like it. It often ends up feeling like a big sham.

In many organizations customer service is broken and almost beyond repair. These businesses view customer service as simply one of the necessary evils of conducting business and selling their content. Many companies actually farm out customer service to the cheapest bidder or set up call centers in foreign countries where labor is cheap. The phone is being answered—great!—but are these companies really providing any service, or service worth talking about? Truth be told, we all know organizations that would be better off offering no support at all, rather than the so-called support they provide.

And poor service doesn't just happen at foreign-based call centers. The service at local brick-and-mortar locations can be just as appalling. It just so happens the day before I started writing this chapter, I walked into a store at the local mall to pick up something for my wife. I waited in line as the young woman at the counter took care of a customer in front of me. It quickly became clear that they knew each other. They started talking about how economical oil changes are at Costco, then about Uncle Bill. Then the clerk reminded her customer not to tell anyone *that story* about Sara. This exchange went on for about five minutes. Then, after the payment was complete, the clerk came out from behind the counter to give hugs and kisses—and start into an entirely new conversation with the same customer—while I waited! Needless to say, I wasn't impressed.

Here's an example with a slightly different spin. My wife and I bought a new home. Leading up to and during the transaction, we were overwhelmed by the apparently genuine kindness everyone involved portrayed. The day after the deal closed, however, we never heard from a single one of these people again. The key point to remember is that customer satisfaction, service, and support should be an endeavor that happens before, during, and after the sale. Customer service is the thing that businesses claim to focus on the most; yet it's the most overlooked aspect of businesses everywhere. So let's review the basics.

Why Losing Customers Is *Very* Expensive

Customers are very expensive to lose. Whenever a customer (new or current) walks into your business, you are staring directly into the face of *a lot* of potential value and money for your organization. I don't just mean literally walking through your front door, I mean anyone who comes into the realm of your business. They might "come in" via e-mail or the Web. They might call you. It doesn't matter. Any which way they arrive, that's a customer who represents tremendous potential value.

It goes to reason that every customer *lost* costs you literally hundreds, thousands, or maybe even hundreds of thousands of dollars. But it doesn't end there, because customers refer and recommend new business to your company. So if you lost the person who would have referred additional customers, you can multiply the losses. But things get even worse. Customers who experience negative service tend to tell others. This is amplified via social media and the other various ways our customers are sharing their experiences.

In practical terms, this means you need to find a new customer—or maybe twenty new customers—to replace the current and future value of that single lost customer. We all know it costs so much more money to find that single new customer than it does to care for an existing customer. In his book *The Loyalty Effect* (mentioned briefly in Chapter 7), Frederick Reichheld suggests that a 5 percent increase in customer retention can increase current customer value by as much as 100 percent.

Why Customer Service Is Broken

Many organizations have policies for customer service. The problem is these policies often come at the expense of common sense. How many times have you personally experienced some sort of service blunder with a company where a miniscule change could have made the difference between keeping you and losing you as a customer? There's a classic story from the early days of the Internet that had to do with Maddox, one of the first influential bloggers who maintained a website with the understated (no-ego-at-all) domain name thebestpageintheuniverse.net, which had millions of readers. Back in 2004 or 2005, Maddox shared the story of the poor customer service he experienced with travel site Orbitz.

I won't spoil the whole story, because it's worth reading for yourself.[5] In short, Maddox wanted one single thing—a genuine apology. And nobody was willing to give it to him. Maddox's story is a great example of how one dissatisfied customer has the ability to recount his or her tale to a massive number of people. Remember, this was before social media made it easier for messages to spread faster, farther, and to more people.

Instead of having a customer service policy, consider having an employee empowerment policy. Give your employees the faith, trust, and ability to use their best judgment and make decisions. You might need to give your employees additional training to break them from the customer service policy mindset. Consider, though, giving them simple guidelines and limits to make the best decision for the customer. Tell your employees to do what needs to be done to please the customer.

And don't worry. I'm not suggesting that you encourage your employees to pander to the wants and needs of every single customer. Far from it. Here's what I'm suggesting: You need to determine how far you're willing to go, and at what cost. *You* need to decide how much flexibility and empowerment you are willing to give your employees. In short, I'm asking you to use common sense when dealing with customer service—and have your employees do the same.

The Importance of Managing Expectations

If you want your company to become Evergreen, you need to make sure your customers' needs are met and their expectations are exceeded. Remember, this doesn't mean every customer gets whatever he or she wants, but it does mean you should be willing to go beyond the realm of what's considered "normal customer satisfaction" in most organizations. When was satisfaction ever enough? Customers don't want to be satisfied. They want to be surprised, excited, and have their expectations greatly exceeded. To do this, you need to diminish your focus on growth and increase your focus on value. When you understand that business is not about making buckets of money immediately, but serving your customers' needs and exceeding their expectations, your profits will soar into space.

Organizations can win or lose in the marketplace based on their ability to carefully manage the expectations of their customers. Let me give you an example. Take Southwest Airlines. It is constantly chosen as one of the airlines with the highest customer satisfaction in the world. But why? I mean, really, *why?* Southwest doesn't assign seats for its customers. It's a stampede to get the best seat, and you have to be careful not to get trampled. Customers don't get a beverage during flights, and there's no first-class section.

What's the secret? Well, it's simple. Southwest has very carefully positioned itself as a low-cost, no-frills airline, and it very carefully manages the expectations about the service it provides. Short of an act of God, Southwest will get you to your destination on time. Once those boarding doors shut, the plane starts barreling down the runway while people are still putting their bags away. It's remarkable. Of course, the Southwest way isn't for everyone. But it works for them.

Zappos is on the opposite end of the spectrum, and I'd be crazy to say that Zappos hasn't been successful. The stories about the extreme lengths Zappos has taken to provide customer service have garnered tremendous publicity. The expectations have been set, and there's no going back for Zappos. But just like Southwest, the Zappos way isn't the only way—and, most likely, neither way is your way.

You need to very carefully manage the expectations you create in your customers' minds. This advice should apply to all of your marketing and customer acquisition endeavors—and, even more important, to your customer retention efforts. Customers need to know what they can expect with your products and services, and the type of support you'll offer (before, during, and after their interactions with your company). Anything above and beyond is where the magic happens, but promising more and coming up with less is a recipe for disaster.

How carefully is your marketing team managing *your* customers' expectations?

Determining the Validity of Complaints

Before we dive headlong into a discussion about how to evaluate the validity of complaints, it is helpful to understand why people complain. In my opinion, people complain for two basic reasons: First, they want something for free. (Harsh, I know—but true.) Second, they have experienced an inconvenience, annoyance, or the like, and they want their grievance to be acknowledged; furthermore, they want to receive an apology, a promise that change is coming, and to know how you'll follow up. Customer service can be simplified if we recognize that we are typically responding to one of those two basic impulses.

We seem to have a desire to turn customer service, and the art of managing our reputations, into something more than what it actually is. We create manuals for how to deal with every possible scenario. We hire expensive firms to manage our social media profiles for us (which usually can't be done effectively in this manner—unless these outside firms truly grasp the character and voice of each organization). I've helped clients build a far more simplistic model for determining the validity of criticism. When I train customer service, support, and social media teams to foster brand loyalty and address customer concerns, I train them in one very specific area. I want to show them how to accurately answer the following question: Is this complaint, comment, feedback, or review *valid* or *invalid*?

Here are two fictitious reviews that I created for the purpose of this book. The goal here is to first determine if the review, feedback, or complaint is valid or invalid.

Review 1: We just got back from our stay at The Fleming Hotel in the heart of Times Square in New York City. We were appalled! We went to bed at 7:00 p.m. and our room was loud. Bright lights flickered and flashed during our entire stay. Yeah, the room had blackout curtains, but they didn't block out everything. My wife and I had the worst night's sleep of our lives. I asked the front desk clerk (who was useless by the way) what he intended to do about our stay? We weren't offered anything. Not a free night, not a free meal—*nothing!* Needless to say, we'll never be back.

Is this review valid or invalid?

Response: Invalid. Deciding to stay in the heart of Times Square in New York City comes with some degree of understanding that you will be spending a night at the epicenter of "the city that never sleeps." That's not to say a guest isn't entitled to a good night's sleep, but expecting silence at the heart of the bustling theater district at seven in the evening is not reasonable. Therefore, the complaint is *invalid*, and needs to be dealt with as such.

Review 2: We just got back from our stay at the supposedly "exquisite, five-star" Fleming Bed & Breakfast in the mountains of North Carolina. We paid $650 per night. Our bed wasn't made when we arrived at our room, and there was a pile of hair in the bathtub. The woman at the counter was talking on her cell phone pretty much the entire time we were there. Even as we stood there waiting to talk with her about the state of our room, she took her sweet time getting off the phone! I can't imagine her Friday night plans were more important than your customers. Needless to say, we'll never be back.

Is this review valid or invalid?

Response: Valid. Anyone staying in a room that costs $650 in a hotel that's marketed to customers as being "exquisite, five-star" deserves an experience that closely matches those expectations. In this case, the complaint needs to be addressed in a number of ways. First, management needs to acknowledge the complaint and apologize to the customer. If it was my business, I would be extending the apology on the phone—not via e-mail and not with a response on a review website such as TripAdvisor. A personal touch here is crucial. Second, I would explain to the customer how this situation has been addressed. Essentially, you want to reassure the customer that this type of behavior—or whatever your specific situation might be—is not acceptable, and that you've taken the necessary steps to ensure that future customers (including the one who brought the problem to your attention) won't have this experience again. Third, I might consider compensating the customer in some way. If the customer is given a complimentary night's stay, I would ensure the priority treatment that had been paid for the first time was delivered during the second visit. I would also follow up with the customer afterward to confirm that everything was up to snuff.

The key to successful customer service is to remember the expectations you've created concerning your content—and then to deliver on those expectations.

Responding to Valid and Invalid Complaints

Now that we know how to determine the validity of a complaint or customer service request, it's important to arm our service teams with tools and knowledge so that they can respond to those service requests appropriately. Figure 8-1 offers a simple diagnostic through which to run your organization's complaints, criticisms, and feedback.

FIGURE 8-1

Commonsense Customer Service

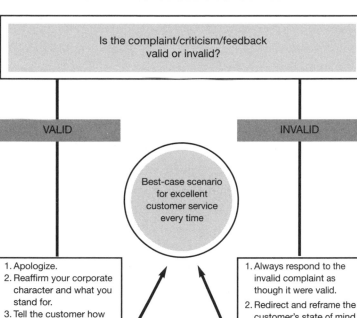

Is the complaint/criticism/feedback valid or invalid?

VALID

INVALID

Best-case scenario for excellent customer service every time

1. Apologize.
2. Reaffirm your corporate character and what you stand for.
3. Tell the customer how you're handling it.
4. Tell the customer how you'll follow up.
5. Follow through and follow up. Make it right!

1. Always respond to the invalid complaint as though it were valid.
2. Redirect and reframe the customer's state of mind by taking the high road.
3. Review the customer's history (if you have it).
4. Don't give free content or discounts in response to invalid complaints.

Invalid Complaint: Always respond to an invalid complaint as though it were valid. Here's what I mean: Customers want to know they've been heard and recognized. Even your Hungry Hippos and problem children deserve a response that acknowledges them. However, take care *not* to give free content or discounts in response to invalid complaints. You might maintain a history of these requests, as Sprint did, but the key is to respond to the initial service request, complaint, or feedback in a manner that is consistent with that request being valid (see the next section)—even if it is, in fact, overly invalid. In a nutshell, always take the high road initially in an effort to redirect and reframe the customer's state of mind.

Valid Complaint: Responding to a valid complaint is very simple. You need to design your processes to ensure that responses always address five key areas, as follows: First, apologize. Second, reaffirm who you are—your corporate character—why you do what you, and the values you stand for. (Remember those key points about your company that we discussed in Chapter 3?) Third, state how you are going to handle the situation. Fourth, clarify how you will follow up. And finally, follow through and follow up. In short, rectify the situation so as to minimize the chances that the issue that prompted the valid complaint will happen again.

Handling your customer service efforts doesn't need to be difficult. Obviously you can do more, but this commonsense approach can be adapted and used in almost any organization of any size.

SCRUTINIZING YOUR COMPANY'S WEAK SPOTS

Every company will deal with unhappy customers at some point during the life of the business. It's inevitable. In fact, most people in business deal with customer service–related issues day in and day out. Instead of asking how you can provide better and more effective responses to unhappy customers, what if you started asking how you could reduce the number of customer service–related issues year after year?

One of the founding officers of FedEx, Michael Basch, suggested that one of the key components of FedEx's success was the development of a concept called the Hierarchy of Horrors. I was first introduced to this concept by my good friend and marketing wizard Shawn Veltman, whom I mentioned earlier. Basch writes about the Hierarchy of Horrors in his book, *Customer Culture: How FedEx and Other Great Companies Put the Customer First Every Day.*[6] It sounds scarier than it is. Basically, the Hierarchy of Horrors is a relatively short exercise that can drastically improve your company's performance year after year.

Here's what FedEx did: FedEx executives created a list of the *eight* worst things that the company could screw up for its customers, such as missing a scheduled pickup, damaging a customer's package, losing a package, delivering to the wrong address, delivering late, and so forth. Each of these eight key problem areas was measured for a short period of time using a simple checklist. For instance, each time a package was lost, they ticked a box. If a customer called because a package was damaged, they ticked another box. If a delivery was late and someone complained, another tick.

Then, the FedEx executives added up the results and ranked the eight key areas from bad to worse to worst, according to which horror caused the most grief for its customers. FedEx then systematically worked backward from the highest- to the lowest-priority concerns. Working on a few things at a time gave FedEx the ability to significantly improve the problems. Since the company discovered that late packages caused the most grief, that's where FedEx focused first, and in so doing FedEx vastly improved the delivery times.

If you want to improve your customer service, I would suggest revisiting the Hierarchy of Horrors in your company at least once a year. It's a simple four-step process. Here's how it's done.

Step One: List Your Company's Worst Screw-Ups

What are the worst things your company can screw up for your customers? Make a list of five to eight things that cause grief for your customers on a regular basis. When FedEx completed its Hierarchy of Horrors, the executive team was primarily responsible for generating the list. That's a wonderful way to get started, but I would also get employees from your customer service department on board during the brainstorming process and give them the chance to recount what they hear most often from customers. Likewise, ask your employees to contribute to the dialogue.

If you own a restaurant, for instance, your list might include things such as the food not being cooked properly, the waitstaff messing up an order, and the host double-booking a reservation. If you run an RV dealership, you might include instances where delivery dates weren't met, customers drove RVs off the dealership lot without completing the predelivery inspection process, and sales reps did a poor job of upselling. A tech service company might learn that some of its biggest screwups include things such as unexpected or unscheduled service outages and downtime. A steel manufacturer might realize its biggest screwups include shipping a customer a load of steel covered in rust, or underdelivering a load by a ton or two, or not properly communicating to customers when a massive load is expected to show up.

You get the idea. What will *you* discover within your organization?

Step Two: Measure the Screwups over a Thirty-Day Interval

Set up a way to measure how many times each of these screwups happens. Keep it simple. You might just create a one-page document that's checked each time something happens, or you might run daily surveys with customers. You might assign someone in each department to check the box each time the mistake happens. Or even better, you might have someone from outside the department monitor the mistakes. The point is to set up a system to measure how many times each of these mistakes is happening.

Here's something important to keep in mind: Not all of these mistakes will be geared toward customer grievances. For example, FedEx was looking primarily at internal screwups that impacted the customer experience. However, all of these screwups also had a direct impact on the profitability of the company. FedEx wanted to know how often delivery trucks were late, or how often packages were mishandled. Each time a mistake is made it costs the company a lot more than a single complaint.

You can really start to see how this plays into the concept of Evergreen. If your organization is continually making the same mistakes again and again, do you think your customers are going to stick around? After all, it really doesn't matter how great your content is if the rest of the customer experience doesn't measure up.

Step Three: Order Your Results

Sit down with your team and take a good look at the different screwups. Considering that you're talking about the "horrors"—the worst possible mistakes being made—they're all going to feel like big issues, but now you need to prioritize them, shuffling the horrors so that they are listed from bad (at the top) to worst (at the bottom).

If you can't decide how to prioritize, don't fret. Consider some of the following questions: Are certain horrors screwing up things from not only the customer's point of view but also an operational point of view? Are some mistakes costing the company far more than others? For example, when I asked a client in the manufacturing sector about his company's horrors, he said that underdelivering a large order was the single most expensive mistake the company could make, sometimes costing the company tens of thousands of dollars (in addition to greatly upsetting the customer). To me, this would qualify as a high-priority area of improvement. Don't you think?

Step Four: Examine Your Roadmap—and Get Started

Now you are equipped with a detailed roadmap for addressing the aspects of your business that need a little fixing. Set some goals for improving each individual horror. You might put specific departments in charge of reducing the number of times a specific horror occurs.

You need to ensure there's accountability for the reduction of the horrors. If one department was making a mistake twice each day, see if it can quickly reduce the occurrence of that mistake to once a day. Also, you should create and accept feedback from those charged with reducing the horrors. Sometimes your employees or parts of your team might have suggestions for ways to drastically reduce the horrors. So the question is: Do you have a system by which members of your team can offer feedback and have it considered and acted upon?

This is such a simple model—and yet one that could have significant impact on any organization. Are you showing your customers a film that allows them to leave the theater smiling and wishing for more—or are you presenting a fright show?

WHY AUTHENTICITY IS IMPORTANT

There's a classic story in the marketing world about "the roach letter." It has gained such notoriety that it even has its own entry on Snopes.com, a popular website that either debunks or affirms popular stories. Snopes says the roach letter is pure urban legend. The events *could* have happened to someone, somewhere, at some time, but the details are so general that they can't be verified.

Regardless of whether it actually happened, the story is worth recounting. I've heard it many times, and it is told different ways each and every time. Here's one version:

> A man boards a pricey international flight from New York to Paris. An hour into the flight, the attendants start serving dinner. The man's dinner arrives and he begins with a beautiful salad topped with mandarin oranges and cashews. He opens the packet of dressing, pours it on, and begins tossing the salad. That's when he sees it! Our poor traveler finds a big black cockroach in the bottom of his salad. The passenger quickly buzzes the flight attendant, who apologies profusely. The attendant offers him a new salad, but the traveler is too disgusted to try anything else.

During the rest of the flight, the passenger can't get the experience out of his mind. Inside the seat pocket he finds a pamphlet about the airline with a message from the president suggesting that customer satisfaction is the number one priority of this luxury airline. To pass the time, he crafts an angry e-mail, which he is able to send through in-flight Wi-Fi directly to the airline's president.

Three weeks pass, and the experience is still top of mind. The customer tells everyone the story of the giant cockroach in his salad. He also tells the part about how he sent a letter to the president of the airline and hasn't heard squat. And then everything changes. One day FedEx arrives with an envelope. He studies it and quickly realizes it is from the Office of the President of ABC Airline. Surprised, and a little excited, he opens it to find a letter from the president himself, on official letterhead. It reads:

Dear Mr. Jones,

I'm shocked to hear of the unpleasant experience you had on a recent flight with us. I want you to know that your experience is not the norm, and we're doing everything in our power to ensure that this won't happen again. In fact, we've had the airplane you flew on taken out of service and we fumigated the entire airplane. In addition, we've followed up with our catering company to ensure massive improvements are made in the quality-control department.

I know we can't change what happened, but I hope you'll trust by my response that we're listening and taking this issue very seriously, and that you'll fly with our airline again.

Yours truly,

Bob Jones

President, ABC Airline

The passenger is amazed. He can't believe it. Finally, a company that not only listens to its customers, but actually does something about it. Imagine—*he* was able to single-handedly ground a 747! He puts up his feet, drops the letter on the kitchen table, and can't help but smile for a moment, relishing the sweet victory. And just then, he notices something. Stuck to the back of the letter he sees what looks like a yellow Post-it note. He flips over the letter and reads the coffee-stained note stuck on the back: "Maryanne, send this jerk the roach letter ... Bob."

This was the moment that our passenger learned the organization **didn't** really care about him or his experience at all. He was simply sent the standard form letter that all poor passengers who find cockroaches in their food receive.

Now this is an extreme example, and it doesn't matter if the original story is true or false. What matters is the moral: We're living in a time when companies continue to set up systems, shortcuts, macros, and automated responses to handle the most important issues when it comes to dealing with customers. These days organizations pretend to be personal and have a genuine human touch, but they rely on form letters and canned responses created to deal with common customer issues.

The good news is that it's never been easier to be authentic. When you come to understand your corporate character and how you want to be perceived by customers and potential customers, it's a heck of a lot easier to be real with those who want to do business with you. When you understand that customer service doesn't need to be treated like rocket science, but rather a simple process whereby you ensure your customers' experience matches the one they were promised, then you can't help but get it right. Are you communicating authentically with your customers or are you sending roach letters?

Remember our goal in providing customer service is to love our customers, treat them honestly and with respect, and allow them to grow with our organizations. Doing so will exponentially improve your chances of becoming Evergreen.

CHAPTER 9

Gathering Customer Intelligence

Examining the Botany of Individual Leaves

We've already established that the majority of companies spend the majority of their time on new customer acquisition expeditions. And while new customers are critical to an organization's growth (I hope you're not getting the impression I would *ever* suggest otherwise!), you should know by now that new customers are, without a doubt, the most difficult and expensive (not to mention exhausting and inefficient) way to grow a business. In fact, I would go a step further: I believe strongly that many companies are literally destroying themselves from the inside out by having such a backward and myopic view of business growth.

I'm not suggesting that you entirely disregard your "new customer" focus. Far from it. I'm merely hoping I can help you strike the Evergreen Marketing Equilibrium that I introduced in Chapter 1. This chapter is all about taking a good, hard, inward look at the systems you have in place within your company to manage your growth efforts with your existing customers. After all, your existing customers are the source of massive business-building potential—and your time, energy, and money are much better spent on taking care of and establishing stronger relationships with those customers than on chasing new ones. For any business, at any stage, this is critically important for a number of reasons: focusing on your existing customers will allow you to create new profits faster and more easily than you would with new customers, and building a retention/relationship culture in your business will ensure that you maximize the potential value of every customer.

Remember, though, that every existing customer was a new customer at some point. You want to ensure you have the right systems in place to allow new customers to grow with your organization. This chapter will help you put the systems in place to do just that. But first, let's address all that money that has been left on the table...

RECOGNIZING WHEN CUSTOMERS
LEAVE MONEY ON THE TABLE

Remember the story about Rachel Brown's bakery, Need a Cake, and its disastrous experience with Groupon? I believe promotional-based tools such as Groupon can be highly effective at driving new customers through your doors. However, as a business, you need to be crystal clear about what you aim to achieve with this opportunity before you embark on it. And (it goes without saying) you also need to be fully prepared for the potential onslaught of new customers. Otherwise, you run the risk of losing your shirt—and in the end not having much of anything to show for your efforts. The difference between businesses that make this type of dramatic promotion work vs. those that don't is major.

I've purchased a number of ultrahigh discounts and have enjoyed most of them. I'm always shocked, though, at just how much money is generally left on the table after the transaction (in other words, how much in potential future profits the company forgoes by not making moves to establish a long-term relationship with me). Whenever I visit a restaurant that's intrigued me enough to try it and that establishment doesn't take the opportunity to try and learn about who I am, or to capture my details into some sort of database, I think the business owners have entirely missed the boat. They're not focused on systematically building a relationship with me. Instead, they are relying on their content to bring me through their doors again—and, as we know, the content alone is almost never enough. Sure, the food might be extraordinary, but out of sight, out of mind. People are busy. We forget or quickly return to old habits. Why not put retention systems in place to bring customers back? It's simple.

A few years ago the owner of a small local restaurant came to me and explained that while things were busy, the business wasn't growing. When I asked about the customer database, I discovered, to my surprise, that one didn't exist. I helped my client create a very simple system for capturing customers' names, and just four short years later, he maintains a database of more than 6,000 customers. Those customers have literally become the lifeblood of the business. The customer database has allowed him to go from stagnation to growth of more than 30 percent year after year.

If you have a small to medium-size company and you're not building a customer database, you have a serious hole in your business model. You're doing nothing short of missing one of the crucial components of success in business. Just as the customer is your most valuable asset, that asset is useless if you have no way to access it. How can you strategically and methodically market to your customers if you have no way to reach them? You need to be able to harness the power of your database. You need to be able to e-mail, call, or tweet your customers. Whatever is appropriate—even send them snail mail, if that's right for your audience. This is one of the keys to building an Evergreen business, and it can't be overlooked.

Many larger organizations now have very sophisticated customer relationship management (CRM) systems in place. Many smaller companies have nothing in place. Still others have all their customer information in files in a cabinet, or in databases on a computer, but they've never done anything useful with the data. A database is only useful if you actually use it. The problem, though, is that many people don't know how to use it—or maybe aren't inclined to because they don't fully understand what the database has the potential to do. If that's the situation you find yourself in, I'm glad you're reading this book. Carry on.

A customer database will allow you to better understand your customers. You'll learn helpful things, such as how frequently they shop with you, when they last visited your business, and how much they spent. And that's just the beginning. Once you set up the basic fields, you can start segmenting your customer list. That's where the fun begins, because that's when you are able to create even more effective marketing based on the archetypes you developed and defined earlier.

The client I mentioned a moment ago continually segments his list. He also lets customers choose specifically what sort of information they're interested in receiving. This brings me to an important point about your customer list. Your list is the most important tool you have for unlocking the potential value in your customers. Your existing and soon-to-be customers should be on different lists, as each requires different kinds of messages. When I talk about segmenting your customer list, what I'm referring to is breaking it up in different and specific ways to match different and specific criteria. We'll get to this segmentation (and how to use your list) shortly. But first, let's talk about the various ways you can capture your customer data.

CHOOSING YOUR DATA COLLECTION TOOLS

How do you capture the information about your customers? Data collection is really a personal thing—one that each organization needs to approach in a way that makes sense for its unique character. For example, the size of the company, the type of company, and the nature of the interaction with the customer (online, in-store) all need to be considered carefully. It's also important to contemplate your customer archetypes and how they communicate with your company. And finally, it is key to recognize the range of options available—from high-tech to low-tech—and that each has unique merits. Let's talk about a few of the most common options for data collection.

Old-School Inquiry Cards

You can start a customer database on paper. As silly and archaic as it may sound to ask customers to answer a few questions on a simple piece of paper, don't you think you would be better off with this system than with no system? Remember the earlier example of my local butcher, and how the index-cards-in-the-shoebox system worked for that business? Yes, you would also benefit from this system (if it is right for your character).

I know many companies that use something as simple as a comment card for the main purpose of collecting customer information. Sure, they're also interested in gaining their customers' feedback and learning about individual customer's experiences, but the main goal of offering comment cards is to build the customer database. Anytime I visit a restaurant or service provider that doesn't take a moment to try and figure out who I am and how to stay in contact with me, I can't help but think they are just burning money.

Point of Sale (POS) Systems

Many companies use a point of sale system, which might be as simple as a computer that captures numerous details about the transaction. Although somewhat antiquated, these systems can be invaluable, particularly for small businesses. The beauty of using a POS system is that it allows you to track an individual customer's purchasing habits (e.g., dates of purchases, frequency of purchases, transaction size), which we're going to talk about shortly.

The traditional POS machine has seen major advancements in the past few years with the advent of new technologies that essentially give anyone with a mobile phone a personal POS system. Jack Dorsey, the founder of Twitter, launched Square in 2010. Square is a small reader device that plugs into the headphone jack of any iPhone, Android smartphone, or tablet, turning that device into a credit card processing machine. This new technology has been embraced by all sorts of businesses—from the food truck on the corner to the vendor at the farmer's market. Square offers a merchant a back-end or administrative panel for building a product catalog, managing sales activities, generating reports, and sending promotions to customers.

The Square reader is free, by the way. You only pay a credit card processing fee, and if your business is still operating with a simple barebones cash register, this system would be a great way to start managing your transactions and sales activity.

Automation Software

The Internet and cloud computing applications have given many companies the ability to do some incredible things. Dozens of new automation software programs are offered each year, ranging from sales and marketing tools to customer relationship management tools. Some of these tools are tailored to the needs of sales representatives, allowing them to track prospects and where they are within the sales cycle. However, many can also be wonderfully useful for organizations of various sizes (off-line and online) for collecting and managing customer information.

In my own company, I use a tool called Infusionsoft. This sales and marketing automation tool allows me to create some pretty sophisticated marketing funnels. It's brilliant. In a nutshell, people can visit my website and sign up to learn more about me or my company or to receive my newsletter. Once a potential customer subscribes, that person is instantly placed in an automated sequence. The automation is thoroughly customized, which allows me to create a personalized experience for the customer. I have multiple sequences based on why a customer has subscribed to my site, from which web page, and what options were chosen. The possibilities are endless. If a customer makes a purchase, the automation will engage in a new customer sequence to ensure complete and total satisfaction. All the while, I can—at any time—instantly find out where a customer is within the sequence or suspend the sequence should a customer require personal attention.

Before you get all bothered—"But, Noah, you just finished telling us we shouldn't automate, and that we need to build real relationships with our customers!"—let me explain. You need to maintain an authentic and personal tone with your customers at all times. You also need to treat each customer decently, with respect, and you must continually offer immense value and forbid the sending of "roach letters." However, there's nothing wrong with automating aspects of your marketing to get customers accustomed to who you are (i.e., your character). The key is that you can do all this in a very smart and methodical way. Let's face it. No company will be able to have a one-on-one relationship with each individual customer, so you need to get smart about how you maintain those relationships. Always remember, any automation must match your corporate character *and* be mindful of the customer archetype you are speaking with.

GETTING YOUR CUSTOMERS' INFORMATION

The easiest way to get your customers' information is to simply ask for it. You might use a simple comment card or take a more high-tech approach. Retailers have gotten better at this information gathering over the years. My wife loves to buy clothes for our daughters at the Gap. We can't check out at this store without being asked to provide our e-mail address. Most major retailers have gotten on board. Some companies now offer to e-mail you the receipt, collecting your e-mail at the time of purchase. Apple was perhaps the first to do so, but now it's common practice.

I could list a million ways for you to start building your customer database. The point is this: If you're *not* building your customer database, then you are leaving hundreds, thousands, or even millions of dollars on the table. What more can I say? Remember Nike's tagline and "Just Do It!" Start today. Here's how.

Step One: Be Specific About What You Need

Organizations want to be collecting three types of data: demographic, purchase behavior, and psychographic data. If you have nothing at this point, you should definitely start by collecting the basics:

- Name

- Address

- Home phone

- Cell phone

- E-mail

Before we go much further, let's take a careful look at that first data point. It's such an obvious one, but so many companies get it wrong. Do you really believe a company that spells your name wrong really cares about an ongoing relationship with you? Do you know how many times I've received material for Noah Flemming (spelled with an extra *m*)? Really? Am I expected to believe that this company cares about establishing an ongoing relationship with me if it can't even spell my name right?

And let's dwell for a moment on the benefit of knowing zip codes and postal codes. A good friend of mine wasn't thrilled when he started receiving phone calls at five in the morning from the parent company of the gym he had joined. A simple time zone or location field in the customer database might have allowed this company to identify which customers were likely to still be sleeping and shouldn't be bothered for a few more hours.

Depending on what type of business you are in, you might request additional demographic information from your customers. For example, it might be worthwhile to know their gender and education level.

Okay, so now let's move on to the other data points. If you are using a POS system or automation software of some sort, your customers' transactions are being systematically documented, which means that you are already capturing:

- Date of purchase

- Total spend

- Items purchased

Everything up to this point, however, is standard operating procedure for most companies. One of the most critical aspects, though, of building a successful customer database for an Evergreen business is learning about each customer in a more personal way. You've spent so much time creating your corporate character and ideal customer archetypes. Don't drop the ball now! Even if your company doesn't want to invest in (or take the time to learn about) more sophisticated systems, you can still build a customer database in a relatively low-tech way, just like my local butcher did.

The key elements of your database will be specific to who you are and what you do. Furthermore, every business will be different. But the basic idea is that the more actionable information you can generate about your customers, the better.

By way of example, here's the type of information any number of B2C companies might like to collect:

- Birthday

- Spouse's birthday

- Kids' names and birthdays

- Anniversary

- Pets

- Special interests

Regardless of whether you're operating a B2C or B2B company, wouldn't it be useful to know this type of information? What other questions could you ask?

I know I gave you a big dose of Donald Trump in Chapter 8, and I apologize in advance, but I need to talk about Trump again: When customers sign up for the hotel chain's free Trump Card Privileges Program, they are asked to provide a ton of information, including (but not limited to) household income, names and birthdays of pets, children's information (names, genders, birthdays, special dietary requirements), snack preference (salty, sweet, sour, spicy), beverage preference, floor preference (high floor or low floor), room temperature preference, music preference, pillow preference (airway, body, junior body, leg bolster, synthetic, calm, balance, purify, heal, revitalize, foam), newspaper preference (*Wall Street Journal, New York Times, Financial Times, USA Today*, or a local newspaper)—and anything else you could possibly think of.

You see, the Trump Hotel Collection recognizes that even though it manages some of the most luxurious hotels in the world, the content isn't enough. Those little personalized emotional extras are what make the content that much more appealing and create a customer experience that's memorable beyond just another stay in a hotel.

Returning to my restaurant client for a moment. Hypothetically speaking, what if he asked the right questions and some of his customers had the opportunity to divulge that they were interested in craft beer and special events only? Then he could segment those customers accordingly and build marketing programs centered around those specific interests. Does that make sense? Sure it does! And this is precisely the kind of thing that is both easy and effective. What questions should *you* be asking? What data would be useful for *you* to collect?

Step Two: Incentivize It

This same restaurant client holds a contest every month for new subscribers to his e-mail database. The winner of the contest receives free lunch for a month. There's no limit to how many times the winner can visit—no questions asked. Each month, my client receives hundreds (sometimes even thousands) of new entries. To enter the contest, a customer needs to fill out a comment card, provide a variety of information, and check a box that gives my client permission to contact the customer with regular e-mailings. Do you see how many great marketing opportunities were created with this simple form?

What will *you* give a customer in exchange for signing up for your e-mail list on your website? Think of some sort of specific value you can give each customer. If you sell European-style kids clothes, it might be a coupon that can be redeemed in your brick-and-mortar boutique. If you are an accountant, you might offer a free report called "The Top 10 Tax Loopholes the IRS Doesn't Want You to Know About." If you're a web service provider, it might be a free subscription to your monthly newsletter or a two-month trial to your paid service. The way to generate sign-ups is to offer something of immense value.

Step Three: Segment Your List

Why should you segment your list? The answer is simple: All of your marketing with prospects and customers should feel as close to a genuine human conversation as possible. Just as you collected your customer data in three specific areas—according to demographic information, purchase behaviors, and psychographic interests—once you've collected the data, you should also be able to segment it along these same lines. When you start slicing and dicing your data to tailor your messaging to customers' specific needs, desires, and interests, you are able to curate each customer's experience. This doesn't need to be complicated, but the more closely you are able to match your marketing, words, and ongoing communication efforts to specific customers, the more responsive they are going to be. It's as simple as that.

Social media experts are always talking about the "conversation"— how we need to join in on the conversation our customers are already having, or else we need to be the ones steering the conversation. We can create a conversation, but let's not lose sight of what it really means.

Whenever we create a newsletter for our community, or build a community structure, or segment our list to deliver specific and personalized marketing to our customers, we are communicating with them. So how do they communicate back? Do they respond to our e-mails? Do they write a newsletter and send it back to us? Of course not. Our customers respond with actions. In the analog world, they shop, they buy, they tell. In the digital world, they visit, they click, they tweet, they like. When your customers act, that's when you know you are in the conversation and that you're creating effective marketing.

Our clearly defined character helps customers know how to perceive us in the marketplace and allows them to embrace our brands. Our community structures allow our customers to come together around our brands. The conversation needs to be ongoing. True. However, the relationship between a company and a customer isn't the buddy-type that you might have been led to believe it is. When a customer responds with action, we must respond with value. Customers want to do business with companies that are responsive to them and are willing to go beyond the transaction. That's it.

TRACKING (AND CHANGING) YOUR CUSTOMERS' BEHAVIOR

Right now, it seems as though everyone loves to talk about big data—specifically, how massive amounts of data enable us to make critical business decisions. The problem is that most of the time we don't really need that much data to make decisions that will have a big impact. The even bigger problem is that too many companies are combing through vast forests of data without knowing what they want to find.

Here's the thing: Big data *will* allow you to validate and justify what you already know. But don't get so engrossed with the idea of big data that you lose sight of the low-hanging fruit and the potential big profit opportunities directly in front of your nose. In Chapter 7 we discussed how Starbucks needed the data from more than 6 million cardholders to come to a pretty simplistic conclusion that should have been self-evident. But what do I know?

Your inquiry cards, POS system, automation software, and any other sales and marketing tools that you use will help you capture knowledge and gain insights about your customers. You can, in turn, use this information to create better and more targeted marketing offers for them. For example, some major insights can be gained by knowing these few things about individual customers:

- When did the person first become a customer?

- How often does the person visit your business?

- What's this customer's average spend?

- Which products does the customer purchase the most?

Even more insights can be gained by knowing these few things about your customers in the collective:

- Which customers make up the top 20 percent within your business?

- Which customers have done business with you recently?

- Which customers haven't shopped at your business in the past 30, 60, 90, or 120 days?

The major difference between collecting loads of data and what I'm suggesting that you do with the data you're collecting is that I'd like to help you gain insights and knowledge about your customers based on their actual behaviors—mainly, their purchasing patterns. I'm also suggesting you consider the low-hanging fruit for quick, painless business improvements and profit maximizations. I'm *not* suggesting that you build an endless database by simply knowing who your customers are, when their birthdays are, and so forth. Instead, I want you to be able to gain actionable insights based on your customers' actual behavior. This is the most powerful aspect of building a customer database, and it offers the greatest opportunity for future profits.

The big data buzz is about capturing large amounts of data and using modern-day computing power to sort through it. Most companies get so whipped up by the excitement of capturing loads of data that they lose track of articulating what they really want to learn. The thing to remember is that it doesn't need to be big data to be *big*. You simply need to know what you would like to discover about your customers. Know the information you want. Ask the questions you want answered. Work backward from the outcome or result you are trying to create.

Let me share with you one of my golden rules of business: If you cannot articulate what action you will take based on the data you're collecting, you do not need that data. Start by articulating what you are trying to learn and what you want to accomplish. Luckily, the process is not difficult—and it can be massively profitable. Now, let's take things to the next level.

The Recency, Frequency, and Monetary Value (RFM) Model

Keeping an eye on purchase patterns can be helpful for a variety of reasons—perhaps the most important of which is that it can alert you to the fact that an existing customer might be defecting. This information, of course, can give you an opportunity to win back that customer. For example, if a customer hasn't visited your business in six months, is this person really still your customer? Purchase patterns can be helpful in other areas as well, such as when one customer's purchase frequency is increasing and when another is suddenly spending a lot less. Be sure to keep a close eye on these different signals.

Companies use three key criteria—recency, frequency, and monetary value (RFM)—to determine who their best and most valuable customers are. This RFM model is a standard method that has been embraced by a wide variety of retail and professional service industries. Here's how to establish the metrics:

- *Recency.* How recently has a customer done business with you? Compare someone who did business with you six months ago with someone who was there last week. Who do you think is more valuable to you right now? Obviously, it's the customer who has done business with you more recently. Past behavior is always a great predictor of future behavior. Those who have done business with you most recently are your best potential customers.

- *Frequency.* How often does a customer do business with you, and how many purchases does the person make? Those who do business with your company more frequently are more likely to continue these behaviors.

- *Monetary Value.* How much money does the customer spend with you over a certain period of time? The more money a customer spends with your company, the more likely that person is to continue that behavior.

The real magic to the RFM model comes when you marry all three areas together so that they form one key indicator. Let me give you an example: Your data might identify a customer who typically purchases from you twice a month (frequency), and who specifically just purchased from you three days ago (recency), and who spent more than she usually spends on an average purchase (monetary value). Now, at this moment in time, *this* is an extremely valuable customer, the type of customer who needs more marketing, better marketing, and more attention from your company.

Now what if the same data showed you a customer, or group of customers, who typically purchases from you on a monthly basis (frequency), and then suddenly two months pass without a single visit or purchase? Those customers may have defected. Don't you think it's worth asking why? You can also set thresholds to classify certain levels or to increase where they reside on your Evergreen Ladder of Loyalty, as discussed in Chapter 7. Consider, for example, a customer who purchases every month for twelve months. That could be the threshold that designates this person as being a *great* customer.

There are, of course, tools to help you track this data. If you operate a small to medium-size business, there's a good chance that you are already running a system that's tracking this data. (And if you're not already doing so, you should be—starting today!) The next step to being smart with your data is to use it to guide your marketing decisions. Let's keep looking at how to use the RFM model in your business.

Determining Optimal Frequency

Think about the last time you took your car in for an oil change. Unless you have a new car, chances are you follow a pattern very similar to most people. The little sticker in the window says you should change your oil in October. You know you are two months overdue and that you have driven 4,000 miles too many. But you wait, and wait, and wait until the very moment when it is finally convenient (sort of) to take your car in.

Here's a question: When was the last time your favorite, or most convenient, oil change shop actually reached out to remind you that it was time to bring your car in for its regular maintenance? I'm willing to bet that virtually nobody has received communications from their oil change shop. I haven't. That's not to say it doesn't happen, but very few do. That's just one example. How about your florist? How about your eye doctor? How about your insurance professional? How about your favorite restaurant?

Virtually nobody follows up with customers enough. More important, we don't follow up at the right time. So let's ask the important question: Why don't we follow up effectively and when we should? Could the answer be as simple as we don't really know when is the "right time"?

If that's the sticking point, then let's dig deeper and answer this question: What's the optimum time frame for a customer to purchase from you or do business with you again? What's the ideal frequency for a customer? And, once you determine this time frame, how might you use this knowledge to more effectively communicate with your customers? Well, it depends on the nature of your business.

Here's what I mean: The car dealer isn't going to sell you a new car every three months. The dealer knows that for some customers the time frame between purchases is going to be a couple of years. For others, such as those customers who prefer to lease, it's a shorter time period. But wouldn't it be valuable if the car dealer kept customers apprised of new models or special leasing deals or opportunities to upgrade—regardless of the typical buying frequency? There's value in the content and value in the relationship. If you continuously deliver value, then it won't appear as though you're simply trying to get your customers to open their wallets whenever you communicate with them.

For restaurants, I would consider the ideal time frame to be fewer than thirty days. Sure, some customers will become raving fans and eat at a certain restaurant weekly. Your more typical customers will come less frequently, but are they even considered customers if more than thirty days have passed? You need to be proactive!

And what is the optimal frequency for customers of a hotel? Well, this depends on a number of factors, I suppose, such as whether the establishment is patronized by a customer for work or pleasure, and the nature of that customer's schedule, for instance. But let's consider one scenario: Last October I spent a week with my family at The Breakers, the famous and historic resort in Palm Beach, Florida. We swam in the pool for hours each day and thoroughly enjoyed the other amenities. Do you think we'll go back again next year? We might. But what if The Breakers started communicating with me in August to remind me that October is quickly approaching and to ask me if I might want to consider booking my vacation? What if the hotel offered me some sort of promotion? The offer doesn't matter—what matters is that this is the type of customer communication that should be automated and triggered in your business at the correct time. It's up to your company to decide what the frequency is.

Have you determined the optimal purchase frequency for your business? When answering this question, you should consider your various products or services. Some products might have a very different purchase time frame from others. Do you see how powerful this idea is? Most organizations don't think about this type of stuff. You can't assume your content (your product, service, or information) is enough to keep your customers coming back. It's not enough.

And this brings us to the next round of important questions you need to ask: Why should your customers keep coming back? Why should they purchase more frequently? Really think about it. You need to be able to explain, with relative certainty, why a customer should buy more often. What benefits does the customer get? What conditions are improved?

Just saying that your customers should purchase more often is never enough. Just believing that communicating with customers frequently is going to bring them back won't work. What benefits are added by doing business with you again and again? Evergreen organizations aren't interested in merely creating new transactions. We are interested in building long-term relationships with our clients while increasing the value they derive from doing business with us.

Encouraging Desired Behaviors

Let's get back to the example of the oil change business for a moment. Why do we actually (*finally!*) get the oil change done? Most of us understand that our car needs the oil change. We understand that the manufacturer has recommended it to extend the life of our car's engine and to keep the car running as efficiently as possible, but we don't derive any real, short-term tangible benefits by changing the oil. For many of us, it's simply a necessary evil.

If your company's offerings fall into a similar category, it can be challenging to build customer loyalty. Challenging, yes, but certainly not impossible! You simply need to take the lead on encouraging the behaviors you want more of from your customers. This is especially important if your content isn't really differentiated from your competitors.

Here are a couple of ideas: If your business is built on repeating intervals, can you implement a subscription model? Is there another way that you can lock in customers to come back when they need to come back? You don't have to discount, but what else could you offer to entice customers to shop consistently at your establishment?

There may be other ways to create additional value for your customers when they purchase your content. Get creative! Here's an on-the-ground, real-life example: A friend told me that her local Honda dealer partners with a local car wash. Every time she goes in for an oil change, Honda stamps her invoice with a coupon good for one free car wash that day. She often finds herself more motivated to change the oil because she knows that she's also going to get the car washed. Now here's something interesting. The oil change isn't really an "emotionally engaging experience," but the addition of the car wash—the assurance that she'll have a clean car—instantly creates that impact. Such a small detail can create a positive and profound effect.

There's no shortage of ways you can set up strategic joint ventures—even with companies in other industries—and share value, and also assist each other in creating an Evergreen experience.

Learning from Costco

Costco is one of the largest membership-based clubs on the planet, and the seventh largest retailer in the world. Total sales in recent fiscal years have exceeded $64 billion. At last check, Costco had a whopping total of more than 67 million paying members. Yet this company of behemoth proportions takes the time to use big data in a manner that provides real value for its customers.

A friend of mine relayed a personal and wonderful story one day that really exemplified the power of targeted customer communications based on buying habits and data intelligence. She and her husband had been members of Costco for years. She said, "We get snail mail regularly, including their magazine and coupons, but I don't recall ever getting an e-mail. Until one day I received an e-mail from Costco, so I had to open it."

The e-mail had been sent to warn her of a salmonella outbreak. It was the fall of 2012, and she had heard rumblings about it in the news, read about it in the papers, but hadn't really thought that much about it. It seems salmonella outbreaks—linked to foods ranging from cantaloupe to chicken—are all too common these days. The peanut butter she had purchased on a recent trip to Costco had been traced back to one of the sources under investigation as being the source of the outbreak. It ended up being a false alarm, but while things were getting sorted out Costco took the preemptive action of recalling all peanut butter produced during a certain time frame. The e-mail essentially said it was in her best interest to dispose of the peanut butter immediately and forgo the risk of sickness or even death. The e-mail, of course, also offered to take the product back and refund her money.

This is an example of the power of big data. Costco was able to separate the purchases that contained a single item from among millions of daily transactions. Furthermore, Costco was then able to promptly notify these individual customers of their potential risk. But most important, this example shows how data can be used to provide immense value. In Chapter 1, I shared the example of how Kmart knew a teenage girl was pregnant before her own father did; Kmart was using that type of data to increase its sales and profits by targeting specific messages and offers to that consumer. In Costco's case, my friend explained that this was one of the first times she had felt genuinely grateful for a company's communications. That e-mail provided immense value to her and her family.

Are you starting to see ways that you might use data to provide additional value to your customers? I hope so.

CHAPTER 10

Bringing Back Lost Customers

Bringing Wilted Leaves Back to Life

You wouldn't expect a business lesson to be learned from colonoscopies, but in the book titled *Authentic Happiness: Using the New Positive Psychology to Realize Your Potential for Lasting Fulfillment*, Dr. Martin Seligman writes about a medical experiment that elucidates a powerful business lesson.

> [In one experiment], 682 patients were randomly assigned to either the usual colonoscopy or to a procedure in which one extra minute was added on at the end, but with the colonoscope not moving. A stationary colonoscope provides a less uncomfortable final minute than what went before, but it does add one extra minute of discomfort. The added minute means, of course, that this group gets more total pain than the routine group. Because their experience ends relatively well, however, their memory of the episode is much rosier and, astonishingly, they are more willing to undergo the procedure again than the routine group. In your own life, you should take particular care with endings, for their color will forever tinge your memory of the entire relationship and your willingness to reenter it.[1]

Seligman is a psychology professor at the University of Pennsylvania, so he may not have caught the ramifications of this study to the world of business. However, it offers us one of the most powerful lessons of all. What we can learn from this study is that the way the customer relationship ends is almost as important as how it starts in the first place, because it directly increases the chances that the customer will reenter the relationship. Rarely, though, do we focus on ending our customer relationships—and, more important, on how to bring those customers back if they do leave.

This chapter is primarily about three important yet often overlooked aspects of business. First, how to identify when the customer relationship is over; second, how to ensure that the ending is as positive as possible; and, finally, how to bring lost customers back. This process starts with asking a simple question: How do you know when you've lost a customer?

Welcome to one of my favorite topics: the art of customer reactivation. Why customers leave and how to bring them back is one of the most misunderstood problems for organizations everywhere. It's also one of the most profitable areas for companies to focus on—particularly since bringing back a lost customer is less costly than getting a new one.

In this chapter, I'll look at methods that you can use to determine when a customer should be put in the "lost" pile. I'll explain the four main reasons customers leave or stop doing business with you, and I'll provide a few ways for you to bring lost customers back, or at the very least to leave them with a positive impression so that they don't feel the need to spread any negative word-of-mouth about your company. Most marketing books don't touch these types of discussions because they aren't "sexy" enough. But I've helped numerous small-business clients generate upward of $70,000 from a single reactivation campaign, and substantially more for larger companies. Skimping on these important topics, frankly, simply doesn't make good business sense.

IDENTIFYING WHEN THE
CUSTOMER RELATIONSHIP IS OVER

Unless your business runs on a continuity-billing model (in other words, you receive recurring payments from your customers, as do cell phone providers, utilities, and subscription services), it can be almost impossible for many businesses to determine just when a customer is "lost." Consider the example of a clothing retailer. If somebody buys a pair of pants from you on January 1, is that person still counted as a customer if she hasn't made another purchase by March 15? June 24? December 10? What if it has been years since the last purchase?

Now let's consider a few examples outside of retail: How about a customer who ate dinner at your restaurant three months ago? Is he still a customer? What about the customer who hasn't logged into your iPhone app for seven months? Is she still a customer? How about the customer who missed his scheduled appointment and now isn't answering your calls?

When should you consider putting a customer in the lost pile? For a business interested in building long-term relationships with its customers, this is one of the most challenging questions to answer. It can be very hard to determine the precise moment when somebody stops being a customer. However, the hard, cold fact is that not every person who has done business with your organization at some point should still be considered a customer. Yet most companies spend the same amount of money marketing to someone who did a transaction with them six years ago as they do someone who did a transaction six months, six weeks, or even six minutes ago. This is a big mistake.

Someone is only a customer based on his or her last interaction with your business. *That's it*. That's why it is up to you to maintain, foster, and build the relationship. At any time after the moment of purchase or transaction, you need to be aware that your "today customers" may be going elsewhere. This is why reactivation and bringing lost customers back is one of the most important strategic profit centers for any organization.

Defining a "Lost" Customer for Your Business

A customer should be considered "lost" when that person has purchased from your business in the past but has not returned when you expected. So ... when, exactly, *do* you expect your customer back? That's the proverbial $64,000 question, and the one that each organization must answer for itself. This isn't a one-size-fits-all situation. Each industry operates on a different time frame. For example, a restaurant owner who hasn't seen a customer in the past thirty days should consider that customer lost and take massive action to bring the customer back. The dentist should consider a customer lost if he hasn't returned for the six-month checkup. The accountant might consider a customer lost if she isn't in touch at the regular tax-filing cycle—either quarterly or annually. You need to decide when the customer is considered lost in your organization or industry.

Segmenting Your Customer Base

There are six main types of customers, as detailed below. To help you determine which customers are "lost," it might help to survey the complete landscape and to articulate the criteria that justify a customer being in each category. Another benefit of segmenting your customer base in this manner is that it can help you tailor your communication efforts, since each of these customer groups requires very different, unique, and specialized marketing.

- *Prospects.* These are people who are considering buying from you. You may be going after them or they may come to you. Regardless, they're not customers yet.

- *New Customers.* They've made the decision to purchase your content. Congrats, they're now considered customers!

- *Defecting Customers.* The moment after a purchase has been made, you are essentially already dealing with a defecting customer. Now, I know you might be saying to yourself,

A Screwup

Maybe you (or a staff member) did or said something to offend the customer. Maybe the customer saw something in your organization that just didn't sit right. Maybe you were terse one day; maybe a staff member was rude; maybe somebody didn't reply to an e-mail in a timely fashion, or the message was interpreted as having a condescending or negative tone. Maybe the wrong products were delivered, or the order was short. Perhaps the blunder cost another company millions of dollars. Whatever it was, the responsibility is yours.

These situations would all be considered screwups and the worst way to lose a customer. The good news is that this type of attrition is fairly rare. And if it's not—if you are routinely rude to customers, hire mean or discourteous staff, flub orders on a regular basis, and take weeks to get back to customers when they contact you—well, then maybe it's time to close up shop.

Less extreme than a full-fledged screwup, sometimes customers leave because they don't mesh with your corporate values, or they just don't like you (or vice versa). The customer does not match any of your ideal customer archetypes and therefore the conversation between your corporate character and this particular customer is just awkward—like a date gone bad. In these cases, there's nothing that you can change. Sometimes, you just have to be content with the fact that you'll never have to deal with this particular customer again. Be glad that the customer left rather than stayed on and caused discord.

External Circumstances

Things happen. Customers get sick. They move. They lose their jobs, or something else occurs. They even die. As uncomfortable and unfortunate as this type of customer attrition is, there are many legitimate reasons why a person may stop doing business with you.

I'm sure it's not news to you that various parts of the world are in pretty deep economic troubles these days. The economy causes big problems for a lot of people, forcing them to take stock in how much they can afford to spend in every area, including in your business. Unless your company sells caviar or luxury goods, and you successfully sell to the perennially affluent (who, for whatever reason, haven't been affected by the recent downturn), then chances are some of your former customers simply can't afford your company's fees and prices. Often these customers can't be saved, but that doesn't mean we should let them go quietly into the night.

Change of Needs

This is the case where a customer came to you for something very specific, and once you took care of that need, the customer didn't feel a need to continue with your brand or your community. This isn't always a negative. In fact, there's still an opportunity for this customer to be impacted by the Evergreen Marketing Equilibrium.

Consider a pregnant woman, or any other number of circumstances where there's a natural and finite window of need. This soon-to-be mother might only need your content for six months. This customer can still be influenced in such a way that she'll help you reap the benefits of being Evergreen. She'll refer you to others and spread positive word-of-mouth about your company. She might even stay involved in the community because of the camaraderie she found. Let's not forget, too, that finite need can be extended with new content. Amazon, for example, knew when I was shopping for diapers. A couple of years later, Amazon started sending me communications about the hottest toddler toys.

These examples point to one type of need change that is based on a specific and justified time frame. There are, however, variations on this theme. In business, it sometimes happens that a relationship ends abruptly because a customer has simply had her immediate needs met and doesn't feel any further need to continue the relationship after that. This is often the case with companies that are focused too heavily on content. Without a transitional phase where customers become more interested in the benefits of the community and remaining part of the overall extension of the brand, they have no reason to stay once their immediate concern has been addressed.

Look, the fact that this type of customer attrition exists isn't inherently bad. It can often be a testament to the wonderful work you've done that these customers have made enough gains to be able to keep going without your help. This is the group where you want to be harvesting your success stories and testimonials to share with all of your other customers and prospective customers.

Change of Habit

A customer may have gone away for an extended holiday over the summer and forgotten about the great experience he had with you. Or maybe the customer hit a rough patch, as everybody does at some point, with work, or family, or any number of things, and now can't find the time or energy to log in to your website or stop by your shop. Perhaps the customer has been trying a competitor's products and services. Most organizations believe customers are lost because they had a bad experience of some sort. Believe it or not, that's the least likely cause of attrition.

The most likely cause of attrition—by far—is that the customer simply fell out of the habit of doing business with you and participating with your company. When this happens, people (customers/clients) always tell themselves (and sometimes you) the same thing: "I'll get back in touch once things settle down a bit." Of course, we know what happens. Things *never* settle down. Or when they do, these customers have so much other stuff on their minds that getting involved with your company is the lowest priority on their list—even when getting involved can be of great value to them.

SOLVING YOUR CUSTOMER
ATTRITION PROBLEMS

The four categories of customer attrition described will account for almost all the attrition in most businesses. The goal of customer retention, of course, is to be aware of these factors, and put policies and systems into place that are geared toward counteracting the factors that you *can* control, which, in short, means two of those four categories. Obviously, you can't control whether people face external circumstances that may keep them from being active customers. Likewise, you can't decrease the number of customers who leave because they've genuinely been helped by you and no longer need your services. (Nor would you want to!) Both of these areas are beyond your control.

Let's move on to the areas that are within your control: You certainly can influence, to a large extent, the level of screwups or perceived screwups in your office. (Remember the strategies for minimizing your company's Hierarchy of Horrors that we discussed in Chapter 8.) Likewise, you certainly can put processes into place that aim to ensure your customers don't fall out of the habit of seeing you when it's still in their best interests to do so. The trick is to have strategic methods for solving each of these two problems—and it's my job to show you the ropes. I'm going to start by assuming that you did screw up because, after all, *nobody* is perfect....

When You Screwed Up

If you did something to offend or dissatisfy a customer—if you underdelivered on the promises you made or didn't meet the expectations your marketing set, for instance—and the customer decided to stop doing business with you, then you have a responsibility to try and make it right. More important, these customers need to know how much you care, how you've improved or changed, and how important they really are to your business. Remember, every lost customer represents a lot more than just one customer. Think back to Chapter 8, when I showed how to respond to valid and invalid complaints and service requests; as you can see, this process is not much different.

If you find out that the reason for your customer's leaving was your fault, do whatever you need to do to make amends. Try and show your customer that you care in a specific and meaningful way. This doesn't always mean giving away something for free or offering some major discount. Customers often see right through that type of strategy. What might be more effective? How about a call from the CEO? Think outside the box. How about a gift certificate to one of your competitors? What can you do—within reason—to make customers realize that you've taken their departure from your business seriously?

Customers want to be acknowledged and know they were heard. An apology never hurts. What's the worst that can happen? If your company screwed up in such a big way that forgiving you isn't an option, you can still try to end the relationship in the best way possible. Keep in mind the interesting colonoscopy study that I shared at the start of this chapter; if the final moments of an unpleasant experience are less unpleasant than what happened before, it will impact the memory of the entire experience.

The beauty of this mindset is that even the most annoyed of customers, and the biggest of company screwups, can be mitigated with a legitimate, genuine, and authentic follow-up. Try this: First, contact the customer and listen intently. Second, never place blame on someone else in your organization—don't throw someone under the bus. Third, present a series of options to the customer for rectifying the problem. If the situation is serious enough, then you will want to refer back to the simple diagnostic process for Commonsense Customer Service, as shown in Figure 8-1. In short, you want to assure the customer that you are taking the concerns expressed very seriously.

A screwup is never the end of the world. More often than not, it's actually an opportunity. When you're in business, part of your job is to recognize that opportunities are everywhere. How successful you will be is (at least partially) determined by how you choose to see these opportunities.

When Your Customers' Habits Change

Most customers become ex-customers because they simply forget to keep doing business with us. And most organizations simply move on. It's back to marketing as usual to find more new customers. This is very scary to think about, and it is a major problem for organizations. If you find that your customers' habits have changed, resist the temptation to move on. Instead, you should concern yourself with fostering customer interaction. The more your customers are engaged and involved, the more likely they are to stay as customers for the long haul.

You can identify this type of customer attrition very easily by running through the following hypothetical (or very real, for that matter) scenario. Imagine, as a business owner or sales rep, you bump into a customer who has been gone for five months. You start chatting. Then, at some point (as so often happens), the customer says to you, "You know, I've been thinking about getting in touch with you again—I'll do that shortly!"

Sometimes they do; sometimes they don't. For the purposes of this discussion, it really doesn't matter. What matters is that it's very likely that until they ran into you, they weren't thinking about you at all. And understandably so, since most people have more and more on their minds all the time.

The important bit is that people *do* start thinking about you after they see you, and once they start thinking about you, they recognize the value they received from your business. When this happens, you can be sure that they didn't leave because you messed up, or because they moved, or because they no longer needed your expertise. They simply fell out of the habit of doing business with you, or it never became a habit in the first place.

Most organizations lose customers for no good reason at all. Things just happen. Actually, the only reason was that their customers' habits changed—and we can, more often than not, blame poor marketing for that. The best way to mitigate this type of attrition is to stay in the customer's mind regularly and often. Depending on the type of business you're in, you want to find some way to establish constant contact. For instance, you might send a monthly newsletter or you might send weekly e-mails with helpful tips. It also certainly helps to develop a strong community. Are *you* letting your customers simply wander away from the campfire?

ESTABLISHING CONSTANT CONTACT

As we discussed in Chapter 7 when we reviewed loyalty programs, we need to be constantly reinforcing the types of behaviors we want from our customers. If you are losing customers because of inactivity, more often than not you're not communicating enough with your customers. It's all about follow-up. Stay in touch with your customers, and stay in touch often. It's not up to your clients to remember to do business with you. Instead, it's up to you to remind them.

The first area you need to address is marketing. How often you're communicating with customers is key. Start by implementing a schedule of regular and consistent contact. Consider creating things that customers come to expect. It might be a magazine or an e-newsletter. Again, every business is different. The point is to begin communicating with customers on a regular and consistent basis.

You need to show your customers what's going on, what's happening with your business. However, your messages also need to communicate ongoing value. Customers don't care about your tenth anniversary—unless it adds value to their lives. The key to remember here is that consistent updates aren't supposed to be about you; they're supposed to be about them. Here are some specific tips on how to communicate value.

Call Your Inactive Clients

Try this: Pick up the phone and call ten inactive customers. Seriously. Just try it. You'll make back the investment you made in this book today, and most likely much more.

Many companies I work with need a lot of help in this area. The unfortunate part is that most of them have systems already in place that provide and keep track of data about customers' purchasing patterns (e.g., recency, frequency, monetary value). The knowledge is right in front of their noses—certain customers, ones who used to visit regularly, are no longer visiting—and yet these companies are not doing anything about it. Money and profits are just sitting there in the abyss.

Make it part of your policy to call inactive customers regularly. You might even consider designating one person on your team to perform this service; make it this person's sole job to contact inactive customers.

Let Customers Know They've Been Missed

When you reach out to your customers, don't just immediately go for the jugular and try to close a sale. First, provide value. Sales teams know they must establish a rapport with a client. It's the same thing when you're calling or getting in touch with clients with the intent to reactivate them. You need to let them know that they have been missed. You might want to refresh people's minds about all the great things going on in your organization, or introduce any new content that has been created or launched in their absence.

Websites track people pretty consistently through log-ins and usage data. Discussion forums often have this technology built right in. You may have received an e-mail letting you know that your absence has been noted. I have, on occasion, received a "Noah, we've missed you" message if a certain amount of time lapses between interactions with a particular site. Again, high-tech, low-tech, it doesn't really matter. What matters is that you should be aware of when a customer hasn't visited in a while so that you can try to be in touch with that customer to say "you've been missed."

Know How Much Contact Is Too Much

Too often organizations are worried about annoying the lost customer. It's a question I get often: How much contact is *too* much? How can I make contact without impacting the customer's perception of my company? Here's the thing: The single worst thing you can do is *not* follow up.

In many cases, you don't really know why a customer left in the first place. There is huge inherent value in getting back in touch to simply discover what happened. In addition, this customer may hold the key to saving other customers. And, finally, let's suppose that the customer legitimately doesn't want to do business with your company ever again. Then why are you so concerned? The only cost here is the one associated with your reactivation system's collateral—whether it's e-mails, phone calls, or postcards. Whatever the cost, it is still undoubtedly less than the cost of wooing that mythical and fabled new customer.

I would suggest the following as a standard template for customer reactivation. I would suggest at least eight to ten contacts (or touch points) over a period of three months. That works out to one contact every ten days. I don't think you are overstepping your boundaries here. Let me repeat: For those who are annoyed, they probably weren't coming back anyway. For those who simply fell out of the habit of doing business with you, they will be pleased by your persistence.

BUILDING EFFECTIVE ATTRITION
ALARM SYSTEMS

Whenever I work with subscription sites I like to talk about the Tom Cruise Effect. The Tom Cruise Effect comes from the *Mission: Impossible* series where it seems as though every five minutes Cruise is dangling from a cable in a room full of red laser beams, each of which is hooked up to an alarm. In your data collection efforts, you need to be building these types of alarm triggers to alert you when a customer has turned around and started to go in another direction. When this happens, the customer is usually letting you know that something has changed and that you need to take some soft action. (Because, remember, as we discussed in Chapter

1, it's never just one customer. Customers often act like a school of fish; when one fish turns, they all turn.) Companies often wait until it's too late, and when they finally decide to do something about it, the customer is gone. This all ties back nicely to our discussion of the RFM (recency, frequency, and monetary value) model from Chapter 9.

Here's a simple example of one such alarm that can be put in place. Suppose a customer pays to sign up for a subscription site. Typically, the majority of customers log onto the website within a day or two of signing up. But what if a particular customer doesn't log on for a week? *That* should sound an alarm. That customer needs to be contacted to figure out what's going on, and why.

This brings me to another important point. Your customer database and customer tracking efforts should also become a way for you to provide better customer service. Here's one such example: A few years ago, I delivered a talk at a conference for publishers. One of the speakers who followed me was the CEO of a large information publishing company. She said everything about the company's website and subscription model was running smoothly, except for one group or segment of customers. This group would routinely sign up and then in a month or two file a chargeback with the credit card company. This went on for months and months, and the company couldn't figure out why. What was going on here? Finally, a manager decided to reach out to these customers. The first person she called was a senior citizen who had lost his password and couldn't figure out how to retrieve it. As she called more people, this same story repeated itself over and over and over again. This blunder had cost the company hundreds of thousands of dollars. However, by implementing a simple onboarding strategy and process for reaching out to new customers, the company was able to almost erase this one specific issue.

But let's dig a little deeper into how to save a customer that's showing signs of defecting. Consider this example: Suppose a customer has purchased from your business every other month for eight months, when suddenly three months pass with no activity. The customer comes back, though, at that point and makes a purchase. Then it's four months until the next purchase. And then the customer disappears. In this scenario, when should the alarm have sounded? The answer is easy—the very first time the customer missed that purchasing interval! You need to have systems in place to monitor this type of behavior.

In the scenario just described, the next big consideration is this: Does this customer match the archetype of a larger group of customers? Is their behavior similar? Remember the idea of the school of fish. This is immensely important. What if this small segment of customers was really the warning sign for a much larger problem or a shift in customer behavior? You need to find out—and soon!

Many organizations lose customers without having any real rhyme or reason as to why it happened, and those customers simply go away silently into the night. Data about a customer's recency and frequency of purchasing can provide significant warning signals. Likewise, data about customer behavior can provide similar warning signals. Set the alarms, and then trigger the appropriate communications. The first and most important step is to figure out what has changed. Be proactive.

Don't wait for the customer to cancel or defect to your competitor. Reach out. Start by asking the customer the very simple question: Are you experiencing any problems with our products and services? This doesn't require you to provide your staff with any additional training. You don't need a manual of suggested questions and phrases. You simply need to proactively pick up the phone, start a conversation with your customers, and learn about what's going on.

From the customer's perspective, you will look like you're on the ball. You've recognized that the customer hasn't done business with you as usual. Customers often appreciate this simple gesture. More often than not, simply proactively reaching out is enough to bring back customers. In this case, remember, you are using behavior as an indicator of change. Something has changed, and you need to find out why.

IMPLEMENTING YOUR REACTIVATION SYSTEM

Do you want to learn how to drastically increase your business? I'm not kidding. What if I showed you a process to generate literally thousands, maybe hundreds of thousands or even millions, of dollars today with very little work? It's possible, and I'm helping my clients do it all the time. All it takes is making reactivation campaigns a standard part of your customer strategy.

Reactivation plans or strategies are the processes we have in place for when we've lost the customer. It's what happens when retention doesn't work. It's our best course of action when customers are lost despite our best efforts to build a relationship with them. Of course, we're always better off retaining customers and focusing on building Evergreen relationships in the first place. However, sometimes, in spite of our best efforts, some customers are going to be lost. Sometimes there's nothing we can do about that.

But what if there was a simple way to bring them back? What if you could have a system in place to bring lost customers back to you? That's what reactivation systems are all about. Not only do you need retention systems for keeping customers, and referral systems for generating greater word-of-mouth, new referrals, and testimonials. The next-best system your organization can have in place is a proper reactivation system.

Reactivation might be the single fastest way to generate short-term profits in any business. Your existing customers are, of course, your best and most valuable customers. Your next-best customers are those who were existing customers but who are now lost customers, despite your best efforts. One of the first things I do when working with a client looking to quickly generate profits—and pay for my services—is to help the client create a reactivation campaign.

Another important benefit of reactivating past customers is that they typically cost far less to service than new customers do. They are already familiar with doing business with you. They've already gone through your onboarding process (more about this in Chapter 11). You also already know quite a bit about these customers. For example, if you've followed any of what I've been suggesting in this book, then you should be able to address them personally. Keep in mind that when you do manage to bring a customer back—and by "back" I mean the customer makes a purchase—that customer is, once again, at risk of defecting. Don't let what happened last time happen again.

Precisely how you undertake a reactivation campaign really depends on your corporate character and customer archetype. You need to use a medium that resonates with your ideal customer archetype. For example, an online retailer may use e-mail for its reactivation campaigns, but a B2B company may call past customers on the phone. In my experience, the best reactivation campaigns use a multitude of mediums to reach lost customers. In addition, reactivation systems are exactly that—they're a multipronged approach as opposed to a simple one-off endeavor. The key to remember is this: You want to invite your customers to come back and do business with you. Regardless of why they left, you want to reassure them that there are no hard feelings, and that you will welcome them back into your community at any time.

You can easily and effectively implement an effective reactivation system within your business. Simply keep in mind and follow these five key steps:

1. Rekindle preexisting Evergreen relationships.

2. Craft your messaging and material carefully.

3. Deliver your reactivation system effectively.

4. Track the results.

5. Monitor your efforts continuously.

Let's take a moment now and break down each step in greater detail so that you can implement these processes in your organization.

Step One: Rekindle Preexisting Evergreen Relationships

Reactivation is so much easier when you've built Evergreen relationships. Assuming you're following the advice I've been suggesting in this book, you have been building effective relationships with your customers. This is crucial. In fact, this is absolutely the single most important part of making a reactivation system work. Regardless of why a customer left, how the customer's behaviors have changed, or how fancy your reactivation campaign is, everything hinges on the relationship that person had with you when he was still considered an existing customer.

Reactivation campaigns are nothing new. The problem, however, is that some reactivation campaigns don't work as effectively as they should. This is most common among organizations that didn't have strong relationships with their customers before they left. These organizations typically haven't yet carefully embraced and implemented the Evergreen concepts and strategies. These situations pose numerous challenges. In short, during the reactivation campaign trust needs to be (re)established and rapport needs to be (re)built. When you embrace the Evergreen concepts, your ability to bring back customers will increase tremendously.

Step Two: Craft Your Messaging and Material Carefully

Write and deliver your material in a way that matches your corporate character and resonates in a friendly and personal way with your ideal customer archetype. Your message has to do one thing really well, and do it effectively. It has to clearly indicate that you are getting in touch with customers because you care about their business and the relationship you had.

Here's an example of how *not* to do it: If you've ever been a member of a message board or other online discussion forum, you've no doubt received an automated e-mail when you haven't been to the site in a while. "Our records indicate it's been a while since you've visited us." Could this message be any less personal? These "reactivation" attempts have absolutely no personality or authenticity. The bottom line here is simple:

Regardless of what your intentions are, if you don't communicate with people in a way that feels real, they are not going to come back.

Step Three: Deliver Your Reactivation System Effectively

Delivery of your reactivation system is related to sequencing. In other words, how you handle the logistics and actually make it happen. This is the area that causes the most trouble for companies. When is it time to contact a customer? How often should you contact the person? If you're a B2B company and a sales team is handling your reactivation system, are they expected to make ten calls a day? Or fifty?

Here's what is usually required: Typically, you are going to need multiple contacts or touch points with customers across a number of different mediums. Sure, some clients will come back after a single e-mail or phone call, but many won't. You need to give the delivery and sequencing of your system important consideration. Every touch point should also have some sort of call to action. Depending on your content, you may need a small series of "yeses" to bring the person back as a genuine customer, and that's all the more reason to consider the sequence. You can't just hand off a list of names and say to your sales representatives, "Call these people." Remember, you need to set up a proper system and make it an ongoing function of your business.

Suppose, for example, your customer has just returned from a long day at work. The last thing on this customer's mind is your business. Let's suppose that within the stack of mail is one of the pieces of your reactivation sequence. Inside the letter, you have a call to action, and the next part of the sequence is determined solely based on what happens from that contact. Let's suppose your customer simply tosses the envelope in the garbage, without even opening it. If this was your only attempt at customer reactivation, you've failed.

Now consider another scenario: Let's suppose the customer didn't open the mailing you sent, but he read your e-mail, or answered the phone when you called. You'll be thankful, then, that you had multiple touch points and didn't simply give up after the first attempt.

Don't rely on a single touch point to be an effective reactivation system. It's not. An effective reactivation system requires multiple communications, often through multiple mediums and multiple steps. (I'll explain these multiple steps shortly.) Plus, as you'll see, you also need to be diligently tracking your results to ensure you know where a customer is within the system.

Step Four: Track the Results

As with any sales and marketing efforts, you need to track your results. I could write an entire chapter on the importance of testing, because once again it's an area of business that is far too often overlooked. You need to document your attempts. What's working? What's not working? What could be improved?

Of course, the most important thing is to track where different customers are in the sequence, and what needs to happen next. A couple of paragraphs ago I said you need to have multiple steps in your process, right? Well, what if you have a six-step reactivation sequence and a client comes back after the first contact? Then you need to ensure that this client doesn't get the next five touch points. Remember, the most important part of embracing the concepts of Evergreen within your business is to simulate, in as honest a manner as possible, a one-on-one dialogue between your company and your customer. From a customer's perspective, it doesn't feel authentic if that person keeps getting e-mails and calls after she has returned to doing business with your organization. Keep it real!

Step Five: Monitor Your Efforts Continuously

I hope you're not getting the impression that a reactivation campaign is a onetime thing. You need to build this system or process into your business, and it needs to be ongoing. In addition, you need to follow through every time.

If you're a small one-person shop, it may feel too hectic to write the e-mails, send the letters, and make the phone calls. You need to have systems in place to make this manageable and effective. I helped one small-business client build a system where every day she could easily handle the process on her own. Larger companies should look at tools, such as Infusionsoft or Microsoft's Autopilot, that allow you to build follow-up sequences that can be triggered to start automatically or with the click of a button. The important thing is that this process should be ongoing, not a start-and-stop operation. It should become so fluid that you can easily manage it alongside your normal daily operations.

MANAGING YOUR EXPECTATIONS ABOUT REACTIVATION

Some companies have misguided expectations about reactivation. One client, for example, came to me with a list of more than 3,000 lost customers, none of whom had made a purchase in the previous twelve months. Most companies would consider this to be a dead list. In fact, most companies wouldn't spend any time at all to follow up with these customers. We, however, built a simple reactivation system and began running it against this list of lost customers.

After three months I was back in the client's office with both the marketing manager, who was responsible for the campaign, and the CEO of the company. The marketing manager said, "Noah, we've been running the campaign for two months and only 140 customers have come back." Now, I've never been particularly good at math, but I quickly knew that 140 out of 3,000 represented a 5 percent response rate in two months. So I asked a few off-topic questions about past marketing campaigns and how well they did. Typically, the company generated about a 2 percent or 3 percent return on its efforts to generate new customers. Next, I asked what the cost had been to implement the reactivation system. In this case, it was literally pennies on the dollars. (To be exact, the company spent about $3,000 in labor and the physical expense to print and mail the letter.) So then I asked what, on average, were these reactivated customers spending? On average, their first purchase back was about $350. It is worth noting that we already knew that each customer of this company typically makes that purchase twice a year.

Then I asked the magic question: "In two months you've spent $3,000 to generate $50,000 in additional revenue. What *exactly* isn't working?" The CEO just smiled.

Keep in mind, this snapshot doesn't take into effect that various customers were at different stages in the sequence; we knew the system was working, and it was still expected to run for an additional month. More money was certainly coming! This snapshot also doesn't take into effect that the company is now more focused on building relationships with its customers; it is now Evergreen.

The CEO had smiled because there is simply no rational way to argue with these types of results. I thought for a moment he was going to tell the marketing manager to take a hike. Sure, implementing a reactivation campaign is not as glamorous as implementing a new marketing campaign. It's not as glitzy as creating a funny YouTube video with the hopes of it going viral. But, gee, what would you rather have? A few pats on the back, some artificial likes, a couple random mentions on Twitter, or money in the bank?

Reactivating lost customers isn't easy—because it takes time, energy, and resources away from the new customer acquisition addition. But it *is* simple—because with some focus on who left, and why, there's a good opportunity you can bring them back.

CHAPTER 11

Bringing In New Customers

Creating Optimal Growing Conditions

One of the most beloved metaphors used by direct response marketers and clever copywriters is the concept of the "greased chute." The idea is that once a prospect starts viewing (or reading) your sales or marketing material, you want to make it incredibly easy for that person to continue viewing (or reading) it, increasingly building interest until the prospect decides it is imperative to buy *now, Now, NOW!* Picture the customer sliding down a greased chute saying *yes, Yes, YES!* The next time you can't sleep in the middle of the night, turn on the television. Essentially any infomercial will exemplify the greased chute in its full glory.

Copywriters and clever marketers have dozens of tactics, tricks, and strategies that they use to create the greased chute effect, and they are undeniably powerful. Many of them are fairly innocuous and used in almost all types of sales or marketing, such as captivating headlines, benefit-laden bullet points, short paragraphs, and story structures. However, marketers who are trying to create a greased chute take their pitches to another level by appealing to customers' emotions, pushing all the right buttons—sometimes with little regard for anything else.

Marketers have become exceedingly good at using their tricks and tools of the trade to make their content appealing to consumers—almost too good! Add in psychological testing of elements (such as headline colors, font sizes, picture placements, and so forth) that affect buying behavior, and it's possible to create ads and campaigns that are extremely persuasive. Many companies, consequently, find it fairly easy to drive new customers through their doors. They are actually pretty darn good at that. It's the steps that immediately follow that pose the challenges—the precise steps that distinguish Evergreen businesses from the rest of the pack.

When considering how your company acquires new customers you need to think about two major components. On the one end of the rainbow is your front-end (customer acquisition) marketing, which is everything you do to bring the customer in. After working through the previous chapters—crafting your corporate character, building your ideal customer archetypes, understanding the role your content plays—you should now be an expert at building your front-end marketing. You should now know, firsthand, how effective marketing can be when you understand how to match your messages to your customer archetypes, at the right time, using the right medium.

On the other end of the rainbow is your back-end marketing. This is everything that happens *after* the sale. The biggest and most glaring misstep that I've seen is that most marketing doesn't pay any attention to what happens at this point in the process. Average marketers believe their sole purpose is to sell content. As long as someone took the next step and became a customer, the marketers feel as though they have succeeded. As long as the sales reps closed the deals, they feel as though they have done their job. These average marketers and salespeople aren't at all concerned with how the content is delivered, consumed, or experienced after the sale. This is a big mistake.

Up until this point, the main message of this book has been related to the importance of forming Evergreen relationships with your existing customers and shifting your business from a how-do-we-get-more-new-customers mindset to a how-do-we-better-care-for-our-new-and-exist-ing-customers mindset. But as I've mentioned a number of times, every business needs new customers to grow. I'd be crazy to suggest otherwise. A business that is only focused on keeping its existing customers would eventually find itself in serious trouble.

In this chapter, I'll show you how to put the final piece of the puz-zle—the new customer experience—solidly in place. You'll learn how to create your own version of a greased chute that sends your customers down a path toward a richer and more meaningful relationship with your com-pany (and one they'll be happy to ride without feeling as though they are being taken for a ride). Once you make the new customer experience the best it can possibly be and build Evergreen relationships with all of your customers, you will be on your way to striking that Evergreen Marketing Equilibrium that we discussed in Chapter 1. In short, you will be setting the stage for building an exciting and thriving Evergreen business.

MANAGING THE EXPECTATIONS GAP

Most organizations exist to create a transaction. They choose to have a simple transaction where the content is purchased and customers go on their merry way, rather than choose to put systems in place to make sure the entire new customer experience is the best it can possibly be—from the moment the decision is made to purchase content through to its de-livery and consumption. However, the best companies recognize that both the content and the new customer experience serve a strategic pur-pose in the Evergreen process. The content plays a major factor in trans-forming a new customer into a long-term Evergreen customer. But, just as critically, so does the marketing.

Believe it or not, marketing that's *too* good can actually increase cus-tomer attrition. How? I can hear you now: "But, Noah, with all of the energy you're asking me to spend thinking about marketing, you're now telling me my marketing can be *too* good? How so?" Because it often cre-ates what we call an "expectations gap."

What Is the Expectations Gap?

When there is a difference between what a customer was sold and what the customer actually gets, there's an expectations gap. It's the feeling the customer has when something was promised in the marketing but not provided in the content. This gap can be created unintentionally through overzealous company-generated sales and marketing, or inadvertently through fantastic word-of-mouth. ("You absolutely must try this restaurant—it was the best meal I have had during my seventy years of traveling this planet, and I guarantee that absolutely everything you taste will put you in a state of bliss!")

Failure to manage the expectations gap is one of the most common reasons organizations lose customers early on. Furthermore, failure to manage the gap utterly obliterates any chance of keeping customers for the long term. The takeaway: To increase your chances of fostering Evergreen relationships, your company has to maintain a careful balance between making your content sound as appealing as possible and preparing new customers for the inevitable less-than-perfect experiences they may encounter.

How Can You Minimize the Gap?

To minimize the expectations gap you need to ensure consistency between your front-end and back-end marketing efforts. Take a minute to ask yourself: Is what you promise in your marketing congruent with what customers actually get or the benefits they receive? Does your content live up to the promises that were made? If not, then it might make sense to tweak your marketing to be more in sync with the content you deliver. Vice versa, you could try to learn where you are falling short and make the appropriate changes to your products and services.

Your content delivery, the processes used for building your Evergreen relationships, and how you bring new customers into your community all need to be carefully considered. Everything should be thought out in terms of "What happens next?" in the life of your customer. And, more important, how do you further the emotional and psychological connection between the customer and your company? If you remember in Chapter 1, I introduced the Evergreen Marketing Equilibrium, which shows the delicate balance you need to strike between "getting the customer" and "keeping the customer." Not only do you need to ensure your front-end marketing is as effective as possible to make the sale and gain the new customer, you also need to ensure that the new customer experience—delivered through your back-end marketing—is sculpted in a such a way that it begins the Evergreen process. To minimize the expectations gap, you want customers to know upfront *what* they can expect from our company, *when* and *how*.

CREATING CUSTOMER LOYALTY WITH THE FIRST TRANSACTION

Marketers typically have a single goal—to make the sale. They want to bring the customer from point A (not a customer) to point B (now a customer). But this goal is misguided. The real goal of marketing should be to encourage our new customers to accept our position and philosophy and show that our content can better their lives, or their businesses, and meet their specific needs and desires on an ongoing basis. We want the customers to see that there's more to doing business with our company than just an exchange of money for content.

Great marketing is about converting new customers to a new way of thinking about experiencing our company. We're trying to generate an intense emotional feeling when customers do business with us. This is an absolute necessity when it comes to the longevity of any specific customer. I hope by this point in the book you realize just how important the emotional impact of the customer experience has become. There's a brief moment in time where organizations have an incredible opportunity to shift their direction and momentum from getting the customer to keeping the customer.

Navigating the Pivot Point

The moment *after* a person moves from point A to point B (thereby becoming a customer) is what I call the "pivot point." You (as a company) can stand still, or you can pivot. Once the first transaction is made, you have a customer. From that point on, however, you have to assume you are at risk of losing that customer, so your stance needs to change. You can either let the customer decide his fate, or you can do everything in your power to keep that customer. Since you've read this far, I hope that you will choose the latter approach—not only to keep that customer, but also to foster a long-term relationship.

The moment your shopper becomes a customer you have a major opportunity. This might be the single most important moment in the life of the new customer. And most companies, quite frankly, blow this opportunity. For instance, if you've ordered anything online, you've no doubt received an e-mail afterward confirming your purchase (and possibly also providing tracking details so that you can keep tabs on the delivery). Typically that's all these companies do, and consequently they miss a wonderful opportunity to increase their customers' level of engagement with the company and to strengthen their relationship.

Consider some alternative approaches: If you own a restaurant, you might, for instance, follow up the new customer's first meal with something as simple as a welcome e-mail. If you have a web service, you might offer a free video that shows new customers how to get the most from your content after they sign up for your service. If you own a hotel, you might bestow a simple gift basket to each guest upon checking in.

Indoctrination really isn't a nice word, but that's essentially what you're doing with your new customer. You want to indoctrinate the customer to a new reality. It's encouraging your customer to think about your content in a new way. It's getting your customer to enter a new type of relationship with you, and helping the person to establish a new way of doing business with you. When a prospect becomes a customer, the way you communicate should change. Instead of trying to sell more, more, more, you should focus on increasing the bond between your company and your customer. You should also be introducing your customers to your community and enticing them to participate. You want your new customers to feel as if they are now part of an exclusive group or club. You do this by communicating in a way that creates a sense of belonging.

The best organizations have elaborate back-end systems in place for customer retention. They see every transaction as an opportunity to create a long-term customer. I don't think it matters if you own a small-town restaurant or are the CEO of a $250 million company. The goals are one and the same. Every transaction offers you the same opportunity. The question is: What will *you* do with this opportunity?

Learning from the Stick Letter

Those same direct response marketers who developed the concept of the greased chute had another trick up their sleeves—the "stick letter." This was an actual physical letter, and here's how it worked: When a customer's product arrived a couple of weeks after the purchase and the customer opened the box, inside (right at the top) was a letter, and it served a very specific purpose.

To the customer, the letter appeared to be simply a nice gesture from the business or product creator offering congratulations on the purchase and promising a wonderful opportunity or experience. This letter, however, also served a strategic purpose—to resell the customer on the purchase and ease post-purchase buyer anxiety, and in so doing reduce the number of refunds requested. (Keep in mind, these letters were originally developed to accompany products that offered things like the chance to get rich quick, or start a home business, and that are typically purchased from infomercials in the middle of the night—presumably when judgment was somewhat clouded.) The stick letter also offered some "action steps" or tips for getting started and urged the customer to begin using the product immediately.

I'm certainly not implying that your company needs to write stick letters to ease the post-purchase anxiety caused by your content. (After all, you've gotten this far in the book, and you know how important your content is. I have no doubt that yours is top-notch!) However, all businesses can learn from these clever copywriters, as they proposed specific steps that, when taken, acted in powerful and positive ways. As we move forward, you'll realize that what these marketers were doing in those early days was really a young form of onboarding—that is, getting their customers accustomed to doing business with their companies.

Every company needs procedures in place to make the sale stick. Let's build out yours.

ONBOARDING NEW CUSTOMERS

You need to have in place a "new customer welcome plan," sometimes also called a "correspondence procedure." Many web services call this *onboarding*—the process of getting new customers up to speed on using and consuming the content. Essentially, onboarding includes all the things you do to welcome the new customer to the reality of doing business with your company. It's a standardized way of teaching all new customers about doing business with you.

The main purpose of your new customer welcome procedure is to encourage customers to adopt certain beliefs and attitudes, and also to get them to start both consuming the content and taking part in the other great aspects of your company, such as your community. Your new customer welcome procedure should comprise two key components—saying thank you and walking your new customer through the next action steps. The format, method, or medium will differ, depending on what kind of business you're in, but the essential concepts are the same.

Thank Your Customer—and Reiterate the Benefits of Your Content

The first goal of onboarding is simple. You want to thank the customer for doing business with your organization. But before you do this, take a moment to think about what makes sense, and feels the most personalized, for the specific customer archetype you are thanking. For some companies, a thank-you note or letter sent by mail might be most appropriate. Others might offer a verbal (and possibly more public) congratulatory welcome for taking the step of becoming a customer.

An important point to consider: When congratulating or thanking customers, be aware of privacy. Companies often overlook the privacy of their customers by sharing welcome messages publicly—in social media or beyond. This can be a huge faux pas for an organization. Luckily, this issue can generally be avoided, simply by being mindful of the issues at hand. For instance, my friend Stu McLaren of WishList Member, a company that creates web software for private membership sites, wonderfully balances his desire to recognize his best customers (as discussed in Chapter 7) with his need to respect their privacy during his monthly webinar. He's careful to only mention first names in his public shout-out, which ensures he's not compromising anyone's privacy.

This part of the onboarding process is a little like the stick letter, because it also involves reselling your new customers on the benefits that attracted them to want to do business with your company in the first place. Create a sense of buzz and excitement. Show customers what a wise decision they have made, and reaffirm how your content will change their lives. Back up the claims made in your marketing by restating the key benefits you promised that your customers will experience from your content. As you can see, we are learning some powerful lessons from marketers of the past. The key, again, is to adapt your new customer welcome plan in a way that's congruent with your character, the experience you want to create, and the archetypes of your customers.

Walk Your New Customer Through the Next Action Steps

The second goal of onboarding is to give your customer a clear and concise to-do list—what we call the "next action steps." The sooner your customers start using, and consuming, your content (and participating in your community), the better. The reason marketers sent stick letters years ago was because they knew the longer a customer had a box full of eight-track tapes and manuals sitting around, and the more time passed before he started consuming the material, the more likely it would be that the customer would request his money back.

You need to get your customers taking action as quickly as possible to avoid any negative post-purchase thoughts that may creep in after the sale. You want to give your customers clear and concise action steps. This might mean instructions on how to start using your content. A dating website, for example, might have a customer immediately set up a profile, upload a picture, and fill out a personal bio. A website that sells a product might ask a customer to join the community forum or post a comment to a social media site. A larger B2B organization, for example, might direct the customer to a set of next action steps to prepare for a large delivery.

Don't assume that every customer will automatically know what to do next. Too many tech services, for instance, think their customers are computer savvy. This isn't always the case, which is why online services should always offer website tours. Regardless of whether your industry is high-tech or low-tech, always start from the position that new customers need to be shown what to do next, and how to do it. Even if your ideal customer archetype is a twentysomething who knows the iPhone like the palm of his hand, don't lose sight of the other customers who are bound to come through the side door.

As part of the onboarding process you should also show your new customers what your best and most loyal customers are doing, and how they're taking part in your community. The same concept that we discussed in Chapter 7 concerning customer loyalty programs pertains here; customers should be allowed the opportunity to see what your best customers (those on the upper levels of the Evergreen Ladder of Loyalty) are doing. So, for example, if you publish a newsletter that you send to your new customers, then it should highlight some of what your best and most loyal customers are doing. You want to encourage certain behaviors, and the most effective way to do this is by showing your new customers the behaviors of your best customers. This is called harnessing the power of "social proof." It's a psychological phenomenon where, when placed in a new situation, people assume that others are aware of what is appropriate and accepted and therefore they imitate the actions of others. Showing your new customer what the best and most loyal customers are doing has the added bonus of demonstrating all the great things that come from doing business with your organization.

I have a client who publishes a monthly newsletter and is very strategic about what goes into that newsletter. The newsletter highlights the community and what his best customers are doing. This subconsciously conveys to those new customers that there are certain customer expectations, and that there is a path for customers to follow during their lifetime doing business with the organization. It also shows customers the recognitions and rewards that come from a greater level of loyalty with his company.

The goal of onboarding new customers, and setting the tone for the new customer experience, is ultimately to create a sense of attachment to your organization and your community structures. You want the customer to understand your utmost gratitude for anyone becoming a customer; you want to show that you're there to ensure the experience is the best it can possibly be. You want to ensure that your company delivers the highest-quality content, meets the promises made when you marketed your products or services, and is well poised to offer a unique and fulfilling customer experience. But there's more. You want your customers to recognize something deeper, more intimate, and more profound is available than simply buying your content.

Remember in Chapter 7 when I described the unexpected welcome package I received from Audi a few months after purchasing a new car?

Well, that was essentially a modern-day version of the stick letter. Of course, I wasn't going to return the car, so they weren't really trying to reduce any post-purchase buyer anxiety I may have been having. However, they were strategically detailing the character of Audi, and how I might associate myself with that character. Likewise, they were introducing me to the Audi community. They were hoping to instill a feeling that's partial to the brand. They wanted me to adopt certain perspectives and attitudes and beliefs about the company. They wanted me to feel that I'm now part of an exclusive group—to feel a sense of belonging. This is precisely how organizations create raving fans and evangelists. But most important, when done properly, this kind of onboarding creates an instant bond between the company and the customer.

Most marketers and organizations make the mistake of thinking that their content is the most important element of their success. After reading this far, you know better. Of course, the content you provide is important. Of course, it needs to be world-class and better than anything your competitor provides. But the entire purpose of trying to get a new customer should always be to create a long-term customer with massive value. The worst way to approach marketing is by assuming that the main point of getting a customer is to elicit a onetime transaction. At the point of the first transaction, or even the first time customers are exposed to your organization, you have an opportunity to enter a conversation with them unlike any they have ever had before. This is your opportunity to invite your customers to join your community, and show them all the amazing things going on—mainly that your content is only a small part of the experience you provide.

COMMUNICATING WITH THE CUSTOMER
AFTER THE HONEYMOON IS OVER

During the pivot point, that critical moment after someone decides to become a customer, you have an active customer—but from that moment

the customer to take? When is the next time the customer should make a purchase? What should the customer do if there's a problem, question, or concern? These are all questions you should be able to answer.

Following Up Effectively with New Customers

When onboarding new customers, it is critical that you ask (and answer) each of the following key questions before sending out any piece of communication:

- *Does the message highlight the actions and behaviors of your best and most valuable customers?* If not, then it should. Whether it contains customer testimonials, social proof, or case studies, all communications should show your new customer that there's more to your company than meets the eye.

- *Is the messaging educational and valuable?* Your ongoing customer follow-up should always be valuable. It shouldn't be created simply to upsell, downsell, or resell—especially in the early days of communicating with the new customer. Don't worry; there's a time and a place for that. One of the greatest challenges for companies is figuring out what to contact the customer about, and when. If you only ever talk about your latest promotion, your customers will lose interest very quickly. Instead, your messages should help customers better use your content and ensure they are receiving the maximum benefit. The contact needs to serve a purpose. If it doesn't, you are better off not making that contact.

- *Is the messaging personalized to that specific customer archetype?* Your messaging should always be conversational in tone. It should tell stories about your company to perpetuate your key character points. It should be authentic, highlighting both the good and the bad. When things go wrong, be open and honest about what happened and why.

- *Are you using the appropriate delivery mechanisms?* Based on customer archetype and customer data, you need to ensure you are delivering your follow-up marketing in a way that's congruent with the recipient.

If you ask each of these four questions every time you communicate with new customers, you'll do fine.

Recognizing Expected and Unexpected Behaviors

Your new customer welcome procedure needs to be fluid and able to adapt to certain customer behaviors. You need to know what the expected behaviors are, and then you must also keep a watchful eye on your new customers, so you can observe when these behaviors have changed or haven't occurred. Suppose a website has a series of videos for customers to learn how to use that specific product; these learning tools are part of the onboarding process. You should be tracking behaviors to ensure the customer is following through on desired actions. If a customer watched the first two videos, but then didn't watch videos three, four, and five as anticipated, something might be wrong.

In Chapter 10, I shared the story about the online subscription provider who was losing customers because they couldn't retrieve their passwords. It wasn't until someone noticed a change in regular behavior and actually called the customers that the company figured out what was going on. (And by then the company had lost hundreds of thousands of dollars.) You need to recognize these kinds of situations and reach out accordingly. If your customer hasn't completed tasks that 80 percent of the rest of your clients complete, then find out why. You might be on the verge of losing a new customer!

PREPARING FOR A (HOPEFULLY INSANELY) SUCCESSFUL PROMOTION

No chapter about bringing in new customers would be complete without a discussion of discounts—particularly those super-deep discounts peddled by many online companies. Discounts have become popular with many marketing strategists lately. Why? Because they are a comparatively cost-effective way to spread the word to an extremely wide audience. Do they work? Well, yes—but only if they're managed properly.

Let's return to the story that we started in Chapter 1. When Rachel Brown's bakery, Need a Cake, was swamped with 8,500 new customers pretty much overnight, it almost destroyed her company. All the excitement generated by a promotion gone viral was overshadowed by one simple fact: Brown wasn't able to deliver on the promises she made. She just wasn't ready for what happened. She was inundated by too many new customers all at once, and she wasn't able to handle the volume. This undoubtedly meant that those new customers didn't walk away with the impression that Brown expected to make, which in turn significantly diminished the chances that many of those "new customers" actually ever came back again.

More critically to the long-term health of Brown's company, we don't know how her existing customers were impacted by this blunder. Remember, the company was more than twenty-five years old! Surely, Brown had plenty of existing customers—*cupcake loyalists all*—who shopped her business regularly. We'll never know the full extent of the damage, but we do know that the promise of "new customer salvation" undoubtedly wasn't worth all the hype and trouble.

Groupon, and other promotional-type sites, can certainly be useful for generating new customers. However, the implications of these promotions need to be carefully considered—and they need to be managed strategically and correctly. The most important thing, something that so many people totally miss, is that systems need to be put in place for retaining all the new customers, and making every new customer a long-term customer. If you are thinking about engaging in one of these pro-motions, here are the six steps you need to take to run this type of pro-motion successfully.

Step One: Understand the Promotion in a Broader Context

The worst (and deadliest!) trap I've seen so many companies fall into is that they confuse these types of promotional discount websites as their sole marketing strategy. Let's be clear about something: Offering super-deep discounts to entice new customers is *not* marketing. These websites should be viewed as a "once in awhile" or "rarely used" tool to drive new customers to your business. They should not be viewed as your go-to source for generating new customers. This kind of thinking will in-evitably backfire, since you run the risk of conditioning the general pub-lic into thinking that a discount will always be available with your company, which will ultimately devalue your content until it's pretty much worthless.

Another thing to consider is whether a "discount" is even congruent with the type of business you run. What if Rolex started doing buy-one-get-one-free offers? It wouldn't be congruent with the company's char-acter, would it? Even a onetime, ultrarare discount might not actually make sense for your company. Would your character offer this type of promotion? If the answer is no, then you need to turn to other strategies for bringing in new customers.

If you find yourself turning to discount websites more and more fre-quently to bring in new customers, this may point to a bigger problem: You may not be adequately focused on building long-term customer re-lationships. Before you give in to your knee-jerk reaction to run yet an-other promotion, take a moment to think about ways in which you might better nurture your current customer relationships.

Step Two: Plan the Promotion Carefully

I can't really blame Brown or Groupon for what happened to Need a Cake. In any event, placing blame misses the point. The real point is that both Groupon and Brown should have known better. They should have had caps on how many Groupons would be sold, and they should have known what Brown's business could realistically handle. When you embark on one of these promotions, you need to carefully weigh the metrics and the ramifications for your business model. At the very least, ask yourself the following:

- What will the promotion cost on the front end?

- At what point will you break even on a new customer?

- Can you negotiate a better profit split?

- How many new customers can you realistically handle?

- How many discounts are you willing to offer, and when will the offer expire?

As with any type of promotion or marketing venture, you need to focus on reality and set realistic expectations so that you do not end up letting customers down.

Step Three: Be Ready to Capture New Customer Information

Since we've already discussed the importance of data capture at length, I won't go through all of the nitty-gritty again. (If you need a refresher about how to gather customer intelligence, and why, just go back to Chapter 9—it's all there.)

What I will say, however, is that typically these promotional-type websites don't provide businesses with personal information about the customers. You typically get a name and that's about it. In short, don't expect to have the data capture process done for you. Be prepared to capture the information about every new customer yourself so that you can implement your new customer welcome procedures.

Step Four: Prepare Your Staff

When my clients have run these types of promotions, they generally do a very good job of preparing their staff for the more practical aspects that the influx of new customers will have on the business. That's not the challenge. The biggest challenge I've seen (and I've seen it over and over again) is that staff is typically not well trained on the emotional part of the equation. Staff members, if not directed otherwise, tend to view someone with a discount as a different (read: lesser) type of customer. Consequently, these customers can, at times, be treated very poorly. It happens—and then, seriously, *what's the point?* Why did you go through all the effort (and cost) to bring in new customers, only to have them walk away with a less-than-stellar impression of your company? Don't let this happen in your business.

At the root of this problem is the fact that many of these teams weren't focused on the true value of a new customer or well versed in the character of the organization. You need to address these issues with your staff members. In addition, you can do a number of things to maximize the value of the customer's first visit. For instance, train your team to recognize the right time to upsell your content. Make sure that your staff understands your high-profit-margin products and encourages new customers to try them.

Step Five: Remember the End Goal

The goal isn't to get a flood of new customers, like Brown did. Rather, the goal is to get customers you can build long-term Evergreen relationships with. It is your job to ensure that you do everything within your power to make the new customer's first experience the best it possibly can be. Only then do you increase the odds that this new customer will become a regular customer with long-term value.

Only by spending the time needed to carefully consider each step of the process for this type of "new customer" can you be fully prepared to deal with the customers when they arrive. Every new customer presents such an opportunity—whether the customer comes to your business through a promotion, or a direct referral, or strong word-of-mouth marketing. Be sure to never forget the end goal.

Step Six: Take Good Care of Your Existing Customers

No matter what you do, your existing customers will know that you are offering heavy discounts. You would be foolish to think they won't notice. Likewise, you would be foolish to think that it won't have some impact of them—and how they view your company. Remember how strongly Starbucks loyalists reacted to the company's efforts to turn low-value customers into high-value customers? There is a natural tendency for customers to think: *But what about me? I've been loyal and I've been paying full price. Don't I get anything for my loyalty?*

Recognize that this reaction is going to happen—and take preemptive measures that will minimize any damage. There are a number of ways to handle this dynamic, and ultimately you'll need to take the approach that works best for your company. Here's one approach to consider: Inform your existing customers of the promotion yourself, and perhaps even suggest that they try and snag one of the discounts while they're available. Maybe run a special promotion just for existing customers. Consider suggesting to longtime customers that, since they love your company so much, they should refer someone they know to your new promotion.

You know the feeling when you find out about something from someone else and you wonder why the person who *should* have told you, *didn't* tell you? It's exactly the same thing here. Don't ever embark on a promotion, with the intention to tempt new customers, at the expense of creating a less-than-desirable reaction with your existing customer base. The gains aren't worth the potential losses.

* * *

It may seem a bit counterintuitive for a marketing book to wait until the last chapter to focus on the nitty-gritty of getting new customers (not to mention waiting until the last few paragraphs to focus on running a proper promotion!). But with the Evergreen strategic approach to marketing, this is precisely where these concepts belong. You see, if you've been reading carefully, you know that, in fact, this whole book has been about getting customers. When you embrace the concepts of the Three Cs, you can't help but get (and keep) customers—and grow your company exponentially.

They used to say retention is boring and acquisition is sexy; if you've read this far, then you've seen just how "sexy" keeping customers can be. Not only that, it can be tremendously fulfilling as well, to say the least. Too often organizations miss the single most important and profitable component of long-term, sustainable growth because they are struggling with the "new customer addiction." It is often said that the first step in overcoming a problem is admitting the addiction.

We've really come full circle in these eleven chapters—and I hope I've opened your eyes to this new operating paradigm available to your organization. Just like an addict who is being checked out of rehab, you can say good-bye to an old way of life and greet the rest of your new life with open arms.

I have just a few more important words to share with you, in the afterword, before you go on to grow your business.

The End Is the Beginning

Shortly before his death in 1992, Sam Walton wrote *Made in America: My Story*, which described the early days and subsequent growth of the Wal-Mart empire. One of the sections that has always stuck with me can be found about two-thirds into the book, in a chapter fittingly called "Making the Customer Number One." In it, both Walton and Don Soderquist (Wal-Mart's COO at the time, and formerly the CEO of the Ben Franklin chain of five-and-dime stores, which went head-to-head with Wal-Mart in its early years) offer their opinions on how local businesses can compete with Wal-Mart. After more than twenty years, Walton's advice is still extremely useful for any business:

> It doesn't make any sense to try to underprice Wal-Mart on something like toothpaste. That's not what the customer is looking to a small store for anyway. Most independents are best off, I think, doing what I prided myself on doing for so many years as a storekeeper: getting out on the floor and meeting every one of the customers. Let them know how much you appreciate them, and ring that cash register yourself. That little personal touch is so important for an independent merchant

because no matter how hard Wal-Mart tries to duplicate it—and we try awfully hard—we can't really do it.[1]

Soderquist was a little more harsh:

If you're a merchant with no competition, you can charge high prices, open late, close early, and shut down on Wednesday and Saturday afternoons. You can do exactly what you've always done and probably be just fine. But when competition comes along, don't expect your customers to stick with you for old times' sake.[2]

They were talking almost exclusively about content. Your content is an insufficient condition for the long-term success of your organization. Essentially, they were saying that when Wal-Mart rolls into town, you better be ready to compete on an entirely different level. It's surprising to think that the guys running the cheapest place in town were willing to provide valid advice on how to compete with them. But heed their advice: Don't just expect your customers to stick around with you for old times' sake. This couldn't be more true today, as suddenly competition is global and available 24/7.

Wal-Mart isn't a very customer-centric organization. It is the very best at what it does, which is to offer the lowest price on an enormous selection of items through economies of scale and state-of-the-art logistics. What it does *not* do is segment its customer base, selectively target the customers most likely to produce high profits, set up automatic triggers to entice flagging customers back to its stores, create reactivation campaigns, nurture mini-communities around its content, or any number of other things that Wal-Mart could do to personalize its operations. Wal-Mart doesn't have to, and it never will. But that doesn't mean that you don't.

The good news is that it's never been simpler to set up the systems that I've discussed in this book. There is no excuse—even if you run a mom-and-pop operation—for not tracking some element of your customers' behaviors, and using that information to communicate more efficiently with those who need it the most. There's no excuse for you not to be building the structures of a community (regardless of your company's type, industry, and size), or for you not to have a more definitive understanding of your customer archetypes (regardless of what your current customer profiles look like). There's no excuse for you not to be constantly reaching out to your customers and looking for ways to increase their involvement and level of engagement with your organization.

That said, even if you decide to ignore much of the advice that I've offered in this book, please heed this one suggestion: Let the Three Cs sink into your psyche as the foundation of how you do business moving forward and how you communicate with your customers (and the rest of the world). If you do this, you *will* dramatically change your company and the future success of your organization. Truly!

Larger organizations can afford to set up ever-more sophisticated systems and collect more customer data, though in many ways the complexity can become a burden. As we've seen, it is easy to drown in data, and that makes it harder to determine appropriate tactics and strategies that will support your character, community, and content (and the larger role these concepts play). In many cases, the most profitable thing larger organizations can do is to ask simple questions from their teams and begin building from there. The salient challenge is for management to take a more active interest in keeping customers (beyond the lip service assertion of providing "*wow* service") and to understand the factors that can and will enhance their ability to do so—mainly the Three Cs.

I'd be naive to think you've never before considered the concepts discussed in this book, and that's not me. The Three Cs is simply a new way of thinking about how you take care of your existing business and market yourself, in a way that considers long-term relationships with customers as being the ultimate strategy. The Three Cs approach recognizes the actual value of your most valuable asset. It's not just a cosmetic gloss of "customer focus."

Even though many of you already know about the importance of customer lifetime value, and most of you have a good idea who your ideal customer is, far too often I meet with clients who neglect some of the most basic questions that I've asked you to ponder in this book. The CEOs and executives I meet know the importance of customer value, and know their loyalty programs could be more effective, and know they're speaking to every customer in their database as if they're speaking to one generic/average person. But deep down, they also know there's a better way.

The hardest part after reading any business book is trying to figure out what to implement or change, without going crazy. I've tried to be pretty clear in this book that—while the tactics are important, and you can build a better loyalty program, for example—your greatest success might be simply taking to heart this one key concept: You need to rid yourself of the new customer addiction and focus more on your existing customers.

That's it. Change your focus. Change your outlook. Recognize the value of who is already shopping at your company and don't dwell on the swarm of customers a new promotion might bring you. Don't miss the forest right before your very eyes, while anticipating what might be waiting for you on the other side. If you must dive right in, then take the Three Cs in stride. Look at your character and ask yourself, "Do we really know who we are, and are we actively portraying that character to our customers?"

Too many organizations try to change too much at once. There's an old saying that "small hinges swing big doors." We often forget to realize how the small changes in mindset or the way we conduct ourselves can often have the biggest impact. I don't know about your business and what you're really focused on, but you picked up this book for a reason. It leads me to believe you have a genuine interest in keeping the customers you have, and you want to maximize the potential of all your existing customers. Perhaps you recognize that your company is too focused on new customers. Maybe you simply need to focus more on conveying your corporate character. Whatever it is, might I suggest that you pick a single area to improve, work on it, and see what happens! And commit yourself to sticking with it. See just how big of a door you can swing with the smallest hinge.

Most of all, I hope you recognize that your single biggest asset in business is relying on you. Your customers are relying on you—not just for great content, but for something more. The paradigm, the way customers do business with our organizations, has forever changed, and we're only just beginning to see what that means for our companies. There's really no point in your company living an existence as a barren, deciduous, or wilting tree. Sure, when the tree is in bloom, it may look nice, but winters are too cold to be fooling around. Focus on becoming Evergreen and treating *every* customer as one of the most important leaves you've ever had.

In his famous speech, "Acres of Diamonds," first published in 1890, Russell Conwell suggested that most people look everywhere for new opportunity, increased happiness, and new sources of business/customers, except the most obvious place—right in front of them, where they are most likely to find it.[3] Too many companies are focused on finding greener pastures when many of them are already sitting on acres of diamonds.

The "new customer addiction" has become a problem of epidemic proportions, costing organizations billions of dollars and unfathomable quantities of time and energy. Each day there's some new method, tool, or platform allowing us to poke, jab, or tweet, with the hopes that we might just poke someone in the eye hard enough to get his or her attention.

I hope that, after reading this book, your mindset has changed. Look inward. Recognize that you are most likely already sitting on all the customer value and profits you need; it's just a matter of shifting your focus. Don't throw away everything you have because of the possibility of success elsewhere. Don't get sucked into the madness of the mythical and fabled mass of new customers. Instead, put in the (sometimes boring) work of actually being successful. Make it a goal to relentlessly exploit every opportunity that already exists within your organization. Promise yourself that you will harvest all the existing diamonds before you go looking for a new mine.

Writing this book has been a fun and exciting journey for me. I hope reading it has been the same for you. But more important, I wish you the greatest success in your own journey to become a world-class Evergreen organization.

Thanks for reading. E-mail me at noah@noahfleming.com. Let me know how you are making out, and if I can be of help.

NOTES

CHAPTER 1

1. Christopher Steiner, "Meet the Fastest Growing Company Ever," *Forbes*, August 12, 2010, www.forbes.com/forbes/2010/0830/entrepreneurs-groupon-facebook-twitter-next-web-phenom.html.

2. "Groupon Vouchers Decision Cost Berkshire Business Thousands," *BBC News*, November 18, 2011, www.bbc.co.uk/news/uk-england-berkshire-15791507.

3. Noah Fleming, "How Groupon Can Save Itself," *Fast Company*, www.fastcompany.com/3001656/how-groupon-can-save-itself.

4. Jay R. Galbraith, *Designing the Customer-Centric Organization* (San Francisco: Jossey-Bass, 2005), p.6.

5. Ranjay Gulati, "Inside Best Buy's Customer-Centric Strategy," *Harvard Business Review*, http://blogs.hbr.org/hbsfaculty/2010/04/inside-best-buys-customer-cent.html.

6. Peter Fader, *Customer Centricity: Focus on the Right Customers for Strategic Advantage* (Philadelphia: Wharton Digital Press, 2012), p. 39.

7. Peter Drucker, *Concepts of the Corporation* (New York: John Day Company, 1946).

8. For a more detailed explanation of CLV, see Dimitri Maex's *Sexy Little Numbers: How to Grow Your Business Using the Data You Already Have* (New York: Crown Business, 2013).

CHAPTER 2

1. Erik Wemple, "Warren Buffet Buys Newspapers. Is He Nuts?"
    The Washington Post, May 17, 2012, www.washingtonpost.com/blogs/
    erik-wemple/post/warren-buffett-buys-newspapers-is-he-nuts/2012/
    05/17/gIQAksMNWU_blog.html.

2. Richard Blackden, "Warren Buffett Tells Omaha Gathering He May
    Buy More Newspapers," *The Telegraph*, May 5, 2012, www.telegraph.co.
    uk/finance/newsbysector/banksandfinance/9248362/Warren-Buffett-
    tells-Omaha-gathering-he-may-buy-more-newspapers.html.

3. Chip Heath and Dan Heath, *Made to Stick* (New York: Random
    House, 2007), p. 56, explaining why a small-town local newspaper
    is so popular.

4. Some interesting thoughts from Hoover Adams on the importance
    of community are cited in his obituary. See Rob Christenen, "Hoover
    Adams, Editor of Dunn's Daily Record, Has Died," *Newsobserver.com*,
    July 16, 2012, www.newsobserver.com/2012/07/16/2202255/hoover-
    adams-editor-of-dunns-daily.html#storylink=cpy.

5. John Donne's "Devotions upon Emergent Occasions, Meditation XVII,"
    published in 1624, contains this famous "No Man Is an Island" passage;
    see http://web.cs.dal.ca/~johnston/poetry/island.html.

6. Customer-written review, *Amazon.com*, August 20, 2013, www.amazon.
    com/review/R3PECWYG0AR1MG/ref=cm_cr_pr_viewpnt#R3PECW
    YG0AR1MG.

CHAPTER 3

1. As of this writing, Amazon is the sixth most visited website on the
    Internet, according to Alexa, a company that provides commercial
    web traffic data; see www.alexa.com/siteinfo/amazon.com.

2. Peter Burrows, "Voices of the Innovators: The Seeds of Apple's
    Innovation," *Businessweek*, October 12, 2004, www.businessweek.com/
    print/bwdaily/dnflash/oct2004/nf20041012_4018_db083.htm?
    chan=gl.

3. Phred Dvorak, Suzanne Vranica, and Spencer E. Ante, "BlackBerry Maker's Issue: Gadgets for Work or Play?" *The Wall Street Journal*, September 30, 2011, online.wsj.com/news/articles/SB1000142405 297020442240457659706159171715344.

4. Facebook newsroom statistic, https://newsroom.fb.com/key-Facts.

5. Catharine Smith, "Burglary Ring Uses Facebook to Target Victims," *The Huffington Post*, September 11, 2010, www.huffingtonpost.com/2010/09/11/burglary-ring-targets-fac_n_712629.html.

6. "Omote-ura: Public and Private Faces," *Nakasendoway*, www.nakasendo way.com/?page_id=1442.

7. "Chefs League Table: Jamie Oliver's 40% Leap in Wealth Makes Him the World's Richest Cook," *This Is Money*, April 30, 2012, www.thisismoney.co.uk/money/celebritymoney/article-2137426/Jamie-Olivers-40-leap-wealth-makes-worlds-richest-chef—Rich-List-rankings.html.

8. "Jamie Oliver Overtakes Businesswomen on the Rich List of Bestselling Authors," April 13, 2013, *The Times*, www.thetimes.co.uk/tto/arts/books/article3738308.ece.

9. "Jamie Oliver FRV Brand Guidelines," issuu.com/bellfrog/docs/jamie-oliver-frv-brand-guidelines.

10. MGO: Proud to Be Boring Accountants, www.mgocpa.com/go/mgo/about-mgo/.

11. Peter Drucker, *Management Revised Edition* (New York: Harper Business, 2008), p. 64.

CHAPTER 4

1. The estimate of 8,500 CrossFit gyms comes from a map of affiliate locations at http://map.crossfit.com. Note: CrossFit does not require its affiliates to report membership numbers.

2. Alan Weiss, "Tribalism Versus Community," *Alan's Blog*, September 18, 2012, www.contrarianconsulting.com/tribalism-versus-community/.

3. Benoit Denizet-Lewis, "The Man Behind Abercrombie & Fitch," *Salon*, January 24, 2006, www.salon.com/2006/01/24/jeffries/.

4. Michael Thrasher, "How Consumers Fell In and Out of Love with Abercrombie & Fitch," *Business Insider*, July 10, 2013, www.business insider.com/the-rise-and-fall-of-abercrombie-and-fitch-2013-7.

5. "Abercrombie & Fitch Turns a New Cheek," *Examiner.com*, November 21, 2013, http://www.examiner.com/article/abercrombie-fitch-turns-a-new-cheek.

6. Anna Prior and Ben Fox Rubin, "Abercrombie & Fitch's Profit Falls," *The Wall Street Journal*, February 26, 2014, online.wsj.com/news/articles/SB10001424052702304709904579406792069595358.

7. Greg Glassman, "Understanding CrossFit," *The CrossFit Journal* 56 (April 2007), p. 1, http://library.crossfit.com/free/pdf/56-07_Understanding_CF.pdf.

CHAPTER 5

1. Chipolte corporate website, www.chipotle.com/en-us/restaurants/the_chipotle_experience/the_chipotle_experience.aspx.

2. "Chipotle Mexican Grill, Inc. Announces Fourth Quarter and Full Year 2013 Results," news release, January 30, 2014, http://ir.chipotle.com/phoenix.zhtml?c=194775&p=irol-newsArticle_print&ID=1895464&highlight=.

3. Christine Lagorio-Chafkin, "Resistance Is Futile," *Inc.*, http://www.inc.com/magazine/201307/christine-lagorio/uber-the-car-service-explosive-growth.html.

CHAPTER 6

1. Robert Lauterborn, "New Marketing Litany: Four Ps Passé: C-Words Take Over," *Advertising Age* 61, no. 41 (1990), p. 26.

2. Philip Kotler, *Kotler On Marketing: How to Create, Win, and Dominate Markets* (New York: Simon & Schuster, 1999).

3. Carol S. Pearson, *Awakening the Heroes Within: Twelve Archetypes to Help Us Find Ourselves and Transform Our World* (New York: HarperCollins, 1991).

CHAPTER 7

1. "Zappos' 10-Hour Long Customer Service Call Sets Record," *The Huffington Post*, December 21, 2012, /www.huffingtonpost.com/ 2012/12/21/zappos-10-hour-call_n_2345467.html.

2. LoyaltyOne Inc. profile, *InsideView*, www.insideview.com/directory/ loyaltyone-inc.

3. Kim Bhasin, "Starbucks Exec: 'We Know Who You Are, We Know How You're Different from Others,'" March 25, 2013, www.businessinsider.com/starbucks-exec-on-loyalty-card-data-tracking-2013-3.

4. Daniel Pink, *Drive: The Surprising Truth About What Motivates Us* (New York: Riverhead Books, 2009), p. 204.

CHAPTER 8

1. Clare O'Connor, "Fourth Time's a Charm: How Donald Trump Made Bankruptcy Work for Him," *Forbes*, April 29, 2011, http://www.forbes.com/sites/clareoconnor/2011/04/29/fourth-times-a-charm-how-donald-trump-made-bankruptcy-work-for-him/.

2. Tony Hsieh, *Delivering Happiness* (New York: Business Plus, 2010), p. 147. This advice is listed among the "Top 10 Ways to Instill Great Customer Service into Your Company."

3. "Sprint Customers Terminated for Complaining Too Much Were Scamming Sprint for Free Service," *Consumerist.com*, July 11, 2007,

http://consumerist.com/2007/07/11/sprint-customers-terminated-for-complaining-too-much-were-scamming-sprint-for-free-service/.

4. "Amazon Banning Customers for Excessive Returns/Complaints," *Blu-ray.com*, August 24, 2012, http://forum.blu-ray.com/showthread.php?t=203808.

5. Maddox, "Planning a Trip with Orbitz? Check the Fine Print for: Bullshit," http://www.thebestpageintheuniverse.net/c.cgi?u=orbitz_blows.

6. Michael Basch, *Customer Culture: How FedEx and Other Great Companies Put the Customer First Every Day* (Upper Saddle River, NJ: Prentice Hall, 2003).

CHAPTER 10

1. Martin E. P. Seligman, Ph.D., *Authentic Happiness: Using the New Positive Psychology to Realize Your Potential for Lasting Fulfillment* (New York: Atria Books, 2004), p. 7.

AFTERWORD

1. Sam Walton, *Made in America: My Story* (New York: Bantam Books, 1993), p. 229.

2. Ibid., p. 228.

3. Russell Conwell, "Acres of Diamonds," (speech), available in its entirety at http://www.temple.edu/about/history/acres-diamonds.

INDEX

Abercrombie & Fitch, as tribe, 66
accountability, and horror reduction,
    175–176
"Acres of Diamonds" (Conwell), 253
Adams, Hoover, 33
addiction to new customers, 253
Air Miles program (Canada), 130–131
alarm customers, 207
alarm systems, for customer attrition,
    217–219
Alexa, 256n
Amazon, 22, 41–42, 161, 210
    statistics, 256n
Amazon Prime, 142
apology, 168, 213
Apple, 43–44, 47, 84
    commercials, 39
    iPhone, 46
The Apprentice (TV), 155–156
archetypes, 111–118
    communicating with, 118–124
    "day in the life" of, 119–120
    defining, 111–112
    different rewards for each, 150
    ideal, 116
    loyalty levels, 145
    understanding, 118–120
    uses, 115–116
    voice of, 120–121

attrition, 208
    alarm systems, 217–219
    categories, 208–211
    and habits, 211
    solving problems of, 212–215
    see also lost customers
Audi, 152, 237–238
Authentic Happiness (Seligman), 203
authenticity
    of community, 77
    importance of, 176–179
automation software, for customer data
    collection, 186–187
average, 23
    issues with, 109–110
average customer lifetime value, 19

B2C companies, information collection
    by, 189
back-end marketing, 228
Baldwin, Alec, 25
Barren quadrant, 98
Basch, Michael, 172–173
    Customer Culture, 173
Bechara, Samar, 48
behavior
    data collection on, 23
    encouraging desired, 198–199

ABOUT THE AUTHOR

NOAH FLEMING is a strategic marketing expert who teaches companies how to maximize their profits from every customer interaction; improve marketing effectiveness dramatically; and create unbreakable customer loyalty. He has provided coaching and consulting for thousands of business owners, executives, and individuals.

Fleming is an expert blogger for *Fast Company* and a regular guest blogger for the *Globe and Mail*'s Report on Business section, Canada's source for breaking business news and in-depth analysis. He has been routinely quoted and mentioned in publications such as *The New York Times*, *Forbes*, *Reuters*, and *Entrepreneur*.

Fleming has taught master classes on retention for Mixergy.com, a popular website dedicated to interviewing company founders and industry experts such as Gary Vaynerchuk (author of *Crush It! Why NOW Is the Time to Cash In on Your Passion* and *The Thank You Economy*), Wikipedia cofounder Jimmy Wales, and Groupon founder Andrew Mason, among hundreds of others.

Fleming has conducted webinars on retention and customer loyalty for audiences of C-level executives for sites such as Vindicia, an online payment company responsible for processing more than $4 billion annually in recurring payments. He has also delivered powerful and practical keynotes for corporate audiences, professional trade associations, and events such as TEDx.

Fleming is a member of Alan Weiss's Mentor Program, and is one of only a few dozen people who are globally recognized and accredited by Dr. Weiss as a Master Mentor to personally mentor consultants looking to rapidly transform their practices.

Fleming lives with his wife, Heather, and two daughters, Avalon and Ella, in Kingsville, Ontario, Canada.